CREATING
A CATALYST
FOR THINKING

Related Titles

Contemporary Issues in Curriculum, Second Edition
Allan C. Ornstein and Linda S. Behar-Horenstein
ISBN: 0-205-28323-3

Curriculum: Foundations, Principles, and Issues, Third Edition
Allan C. Ornstein and Francis P. Hunkins
ISBN: 0-205-27702-0

Affirming Middle Grades Education
Carl W. Walley and W. Gregory Gerrick (Editors)
ISBN: 0-205-17128-1

Curriculum Essentials: A Resource for Educators
Jon Wiles
ISBN: 0-205-27988-0

CREATING A CATALYST FOR THINKING

THE INTEGRATED CURRICULUM

Anne L. Mallery

Millersville University

Allyn and Bacon

Boston ■ London ■ Toronto ■ Sydney ■ Tokyo ■ Singapore

Series Editor: Norris Harrell
Series Editorial Assistant: Bridget Keane
Marketing Managers: Ellen Dolberg/Brad Parkins
Manufacturing Buyer: Suzanne Lareau
Editorial-Production Service: Omegatype Typography, Inc.
Electronic Composition: Omegatype Typography, Inc.

Copyright © 2000 by Allyn & Bacon
A Pearson Education Company
Needham Heights, MA 02494

Internet: www.abacon.com

Library of Congress Cataloging-in-Publication Data

Mallery, Anne L.
    Creating a catalyst for thinking : the integrated curriculum / by
Anne L. Mallery.
      p.   cm.
    Includes bibliographical references and index.
    ISBN 0-205-28671-2 (alk. paper)
    1. Curriculum planning—United States. 2. Interdisciplinary
approach in education—United States. 3. Student participation in
curriculum planning—United States. I. Title.
LB2806. 15.M34 2000   99-18205
375′.001—dc21   CIP

Printed in the United States of America

10 9 8 7 6 5 4 3 2 1   03 02 01 00 99

To Pop

Who gave us the desire to achieve,
The courage to try,
and
The confidence to persist.
We live through your example.

CONTENTS

Preface   xiii

CHAPTER

1

Ten Years of Educational Reform   1

Teacher Education   2

Trends, Reforms, and Practices   2

Interdisciplinary Curriculum   5

    Teaching Philosophies: The Great Debate   5

    The Integrated Curriculum: A Historical Perspective   6

        What Is an Integrated Curriculum?   8

Closure Statement   9

References   10

CHAPTER

2

Teaching for Understanding and Transfer: Interdisciplinary Instruction   11

The Components   12

Curriculum Design   13

    Discipline-Based Design   13

    Parallel Disciplines   13

    Multidisciplinary Design   13

    Interdisciplinary Design   13

    Integrated Day Design   14

    Field-Based Instruction   14

Individual Differences   14

    Multiple Intelligences   14

Strategies   15

    Visual Literacy and Learning   15

    The Socratic Method: Questioning and Problem-Solving   16

    Brainstorming: Stimulating Reasoning   18

Collaborative Learning   19
Rationale   19
Practices   20
Benefits and Shortcomings   20
Grouping Practices and Tasks   20
Closure Statement   22
References   22

CHAPTER

3

Selecting a Theme: Introducing the Unit Prototype   25

Organizational Considerations   26
Importance of a Theme   26
Project Planning   26
Characteristics of a Good Theme   27
Unit Planning Modeled after the Unit Prototype   28
Relevance of the Theme to Teachers   29
■ **Historical Background: The Proper Victorian Lady   29**
■ **Historical Background: Timeline of Women's Rights 1860–1920   31**
Unit Planning Procedures and Guidesheets   31
■ **Unit Plan Grading Criteria   32**
■ **Unit Planning Guidesheet   33**
■ **Grouping Guidesheet   35**
■ **Research Topics Sign-Up Sheet   36**
■ **Unit Resources   41**
Closure Statement   43
References   43

CHAPTER

4

Organizational Activities: The Literature Synopsis and Planning Wheel   45

Constructing Materials   46
Guidesheets   46
Rubric   46
Unit Plan Prototype   46
Women of Achievement Unit Plan—Amelia Earhart   46
■ **Literature Synopsis Grading Criteria   47**
■ **Literature Synopsis Guidesheet   48**
■ **Historical Background: Amelia Earhart   49**

The Planning Wheel   50
  Identifying the Problem   50
  Evaluating the Problem   50
  Selecting Subject Matter Headings for Integration   51
  Listing Content Concepts under Subject Headings   51
  Developing Focus Questions   51

■ **Example–Amelia Earhart Planning Wheel   52**

■ **Interdisciplinary Planning Wheel: Grading Criteria   53**

Closure Statement   54

CHAPTER

5

Research and Fact Finding: The Fact Sheet   55

The Fact Sheet   56
  Information Sources   56
  Purpose of the Fact Sheet   56
  Relationship of the Concepts to the Problem   56

■ **Fact Sheet Grading Criteria   57**

■ **Amelia Earhart Fact Sheet   58**

Closure Statement   61

CHAPTER

6

Designing Instruction   63

The Importance of Readiness   64
  The Motivational Activity   64
  Action Research   64

The Procedures and Appendix   67

■ **Procedure   68**

■ **Appendix A: KWL Chart   69**

■ **Appendix B: Roles of Women Yesterday and Today   69**

■ **Appendix C: Guided Reading   70**

■ **Appendix D: Historical Event Guidesheet   71**
    Library Research Guidesheet   72
    Historical Event Grading Criteria   73

■ **Appendix E: The Step Book   74**

■ **Appendix F: Technology Project Guidesheet   75**
    Technology Project Grading Criteria   76

Closure Statement   77

References   77

CHAPTER

7

Assessment, Integration Statement, and Materials   79

Political Implications of Assessment   80

Assessment Defined   81
Standardized Testing   81
Observation of Learning Behaviors   81
Normed and Criterion-Referenced Data   81

Performance Objectives   82
Content versus Performance Objectives   82
Mastery Objectives   83
Tracking Instruments for Mastery Objectives   84
Developmental Objectives   84
Tracking Instruments for Developmental Objectives   85

Evaluation Statements   87

The Integration Statement and Materials   88
The Purpose of the Integration Statement   88
Format for the Integration Statement   88
Materials   88

Closure Statement   88

References   88

CHAPTER

8

The Sample Unit Plan: Amelia Earhart: American Woman of Achievement   89

Literature Concept   89

Integration Statement   89

Objectives   89

Materials   90

Motivation   90

Procedure   90

■ **Amelia Earhart Fact Sheet   92**

■ **Appendix A: KWL Chart   95**

■ **Appendix B: Roles of Women Yesterday and Today   95**

■ **Appendix C: Guided Reading   96**

■ **Appendix D: Historical Event Guidesheet   97**
Library Research Guidesheet   98
Historical Event Grading Criteria   99

■ **Appendix E: The Step Book   100**

■ **Appendix F: Technology Project Guidesheet   101**
Technology Project Grading Criteria   102

Evaluation   103
Bibliography   103
Delegation of Responsibilities   103

CHAPTER

9

Unit Framework: Native American Nations   105

Relevance of the Theme to Teachers   105

Historical Background   106

■ Native American Nations: Research Topics Sign-Up Sheet   107

■ Native American Nations: Bibliography   112

■ Literature Synopsis Grading Criteria   114

■ Literature Synopsis Guidesheet   115

CHAPTER

10

Unit Framework: Black Americans of Achievement—1860–1920   117

Relevance of the Theme to Teachers   117

Historical Background   118

■ Black Americans of Achievement: Research Topics Sign-Up Sheet   119

■ Black Americans of Achievement: Bibliography   124

■ Literature Synopsis Grading Criteria   126

■ Literature Synopsis Guidesheet   127

CHAPTER

11

Unit Framework: Immigrant Groups—1860–1920   129

Relevance of the Theme to Teachers   130

Historical Background   130

■ Immigrant Groups: Research Topics Sign-Up Sheet   131

■ Immigrant Groups: Bibliography   133

■ Literature Synopsis Grading Criteria   134

■ Literature Synopsis Guidesheet   135

CHAPTER
12

Unit Framework: Explorers of Distant Frontiers   137

Relevance of the Theme to Teachers   138

Historical Background   138

■ Explorers of Distant Frontiers: Research Topics Sign-Up Sheet   140

■ Explorers of Distant Frontiers: Bibliography   144

■ Literature Synopsis Grading Criteria   146

■ Literature Synopsis Guidesheet   147

CHAPTER
13

Timelines and Tables   149

Timeline of African American History, 1859–1920   149

United States History, 1860–1920   159

Immigration Patterns, 1851–1920   179

Index   181

PREFACE

COOPERATIVE PROBLEM-SOLVING AND YE OLDE MARBLE GAME

There are consistencies between parenting and teaching. Every parent knows that children respond differently to guidance, and the key to effective teaching is to understand the child well. Teachers who are aware of students' interests, attention spans, and skill levels are able to plan instruction that results in successful achievement. Both teachers and parents learn about children by observing their behavior as they respond to instruction. Learning begins in the home and the experiences of our childhood stay with us for life.

I was the only girl in a family of four boys. When I was twelve, my family moved to a home in the mountains. The boys and I felt a great sense of freedom to leave the city, but Mother had mixed feelings about the move. She recognized Dad's love for the outdoors and saw how pleased he was to see us fish and swim in the creek, pitch a tent in the woods, and plant trees on the property. However, education was one of her highest priorities and there was only enough spare cash to cover the tuition for Sam and me to go to the city schools. John, Jerry, and Pat were still in grade school and rode the bus to the little mountain school in Ohiopyle.

Pat wasn't much of an athlete when he was a little boy, which was just as well, because there wasn't much to do at the Ohiopyle School—no soccer, no t-ball, no Pop Warner football. But there was one sport that occupied every little boy's time during recess and lunch hour, and that was marbles. Marbles were played on hands and knees in a ring scratched in the dirt with a stick. Everyone had a chance, since size didn't make a difference. Unfortunately for Pat, he wasn't a very good player.

Every day he'd come home, his pockets empty, having lost all his marbles. And every evening, he'd ask Dad for another nickel so he could go to Holt's General Store to buy another bag. Having been a pretty good athlete and competitor in his time, Dad felt sorry for Pat, who was taking a beating day after day. So he intervened. Through this experience, we all learned that there are many ways to solve a problem if you are clever enough to plan your strategy.

Dad brought home a Marsh-Wheeling cigar box from the gas station. We all remember it well—yellow with a blue label on the top. Right there in the middle of the label, right there where it said "Original & Genuine Marsh Wheeling," Dad drilled a hole. A hole just a little bit bigger than a marble. On the top of the box just above the label Dad printed in his unique script, "Patrick Mallery, Esquire, Ye Olde Marble Game."

The game worked like this. If any kid could stand with the marble at his waist and drop it into the hole in Pat's cigar box which was sitting on the ground, he won 10 marbles. (Ten marbles were all the marbles Pat had on that first morning.) If the marble missed the hole, it was Pat's. Simple as that . . . that's all there was to it. By the end of the first day, Pat's pockets were overflowing with marbles. By the end of the second day, when the principal caught on to the game, Pat owned every marble in the school. So that's how Pat and Dad cleaned out every marble in Ohiopyle and became the all-time marble champions in the Ohiopyle School.

It was a lesson we never forgot. There are many solutions to problems, and if you are not successful on your first attempt, a fresh look at the issues and a little creativity can go a long way toward paving the way to success. Dad could have solved the problem for Pat or told Pat to give up, but instead he provided the guidance that allowed Pat to solve the problem independently. Through discussion, modeling, and problem solving, Dad enabled Pat to be successful even though he was a terrible marble player. Learning is so much sweeter when we find our own way.

The author of this text believes that the best way to learn is through active involvement in problem solving. If we want teachers to use inductive strategies that involve interdisciplinary instruction, authentic assessment, and hands-on activities, the best way to teach this methodology is to have students create their own curriculum. We all understand concepts more deeply through active involvement in a creative process involving collaboration with others, clear statements of expectations, and the support of a caring mentor. The purpose of this text is not just to discuss or show interdisciplinary curriculum, but to engage the reader in creating interdisciplinary units of study.

METHODOLOGY

Creating interdisciplinary instruction is a creative, not a linear process. Most preservice and practicing teachers were products of deductive instruction, so they feel most comfortable planning curriculum that sequences a series of isolated skills and activities. In a deductive approach, the instructor gives the students information, students learn the information, then demonstrate understanding on a test. The inductive method is often called the discovery approach. Students are presented with a problem, hypothesize possible solutions, analyze the merit of each, form an opinion, and state the rationale for their solution.

Deductive instruction is teacher driven; inductive instruction involves student problem solving. Following the directions while building a model airplane is a very different task from using Legos to create your own invention. In building a model airplane, the task is to follow strict guidelines devised by the manufacturer. Legos enable children to create products from their imaginations and are consistent with inductive learning.

In this book, each chapter begins with an advanced organizer that provides background and sets purposes for reading. A series of questions are also included to raise students' curiosity about major concepts and to provide stimulation for group discussion. Questions provide transition among the subsections and guide the reader into deeper understanding of the material.

Following the advanced organizer is the boxed main idea of the chapter and a graphic organizer that categorizes subordinate topics. Chapters are concluded with a closure statement that synthesizes major ideas and draws conclusions.

Our objective is to demonstrate that interdisciplinary instruction does not begin by identifying objectives and listing a series of skill activities, but by collaborating with peers, developing in-depth knowledge of the content relating to the theme, and viewing concepts through the lens of both generalization and sharp focus.

TEXT PURPOSE

The purpose of this book is to lead preservice elementary and middle school teachers through the stages of the curriculum development process through guide sheets and activities. Each of the unit activities contains information about the benefits of using the process and rubrics checklists for evaluating the merit of the product.

Roger Wilson and I developed many of the materials and guide sheets while working with preservice teachers in our methodology courses. We reviewed a variety of interdisciplinary models and our students field-tested our approach in a wide range of settings. Our approach was to provide guidelines and research for making decisions and establishing parameters for each step in the curriculum development process. We found preservice teachers to be very creative when working in cooperative learning groups with peers who had similar interests.

University instructors who take a constructivist approach to teaching and value curriculum that integrates skills with content will find this text useful in clarifying understandings of interdisciplinary methodology and teaching. School administrators who are training staff in the development of inductive instruction including performance based assessment and content integration can also use it.

ORGANIZATION OF THE BOOK

Chapter 1: Introduction

In this chapter, we discuss the history of teacher education reform in the 1980s and the renewed interest in interdisciplinary instruction. This information serves as the rationale for planning instruction that links a wide range of content topics that are taught through an inductive approach.

Chapter 2: Teaching for Understanding and Transfer: Interdisciplinary Instruction

The development of interdisciplinary instruction is a problem-solving and reflection task for both teachers and students. In this chapter, we discuss brain research, multiple intelligences, and learning that justifies the inclusion of integrated curriculum in both teacher education and elementary programs. Chapters 1 and 2 create the background for the more practical aspects of the book that outline a framework and strategies for the construction of units of study.

Chapter 3: Selecting a Theme

The selection of a theme is an important decision. To make this decision, teachers must be familiar with the school philosophy and financial limitations; subject area standards; student interests, skill levels, and attention spans; time restraints; and community values, resources, and services. In this chapter, we discuss the characteristics of a good theme, provide suggestions for selecting a theme, and offer guidelines for constructing a graphic organizer that guides the thinking process in development of curriculum. Examples are provided and strengths and limitations of alternative plans are included.

Chapter 4: Organizational Activities: The Literature Synopsis

The literature synopsis enables the curriculum developers to analyze the theme of the unit deeply before the actual writing of the unit plan. Preservice teachers are prepared for this task through the use of a series of guidesheets. Advantages of this readiness strategy are discussed. The prototype unit plan is introduced and used in explaining the procedures for constructing a planning wheel.

Chapter 5: Research and Fact Finding: The Fact Sheet

After brainstorming and constructing a graphic organizer of the unit, completing the literature synopsis, and constructing a planning wheel, curriculum developers gather content facts that are listed on a fact sheet within subject matter categories. The organizational process moves from the broad to the specific as teachers select information that will be mastered by students at the conclusion of the instruction. After the unit is completed, teachers revise the fact sheet based on the learning behaviors of student participants.

Chapter 6: Designing Instruction

This section helps curriculum developers structure the activities so that learners are moving smoothly from readiness to new concept development to application. Student guide sheets and graphic organizers flow logically from these brainstorming sessions and appear in the Appendix. Examples are provided.

Chapter 7: Assessment, Integration Statement, and Materials

Teachers need to observe children's learning behaviors while they are learning to make decisions about revising the materials, reteaching difficult concepts, and evaluating student progress. This chapter discusses the difference between content and performance objectives and provides models of authentic assessment instruments. Progress is tracked on status sheets that monitor academic progress over time. Examples of rubrics, checklists, and status sheets are provided. Instruction in writing the integration statement and listing the materials is provided.

Chapter 8: The Sample Unit Plan: Amelia Earhart: American Woman of Achievement

Chapter 8 contains the completed prototype unit plan written to conform to the specifications discussed in Chapter 3.

Chapters 9, 10, 11, and 12

These chapters contain resources for units on a variety of additional themes: Native American Nations, Black Americans of Achievement, Immigrant Groups, and Explorers of Distant Frontiers.

Chapter 13: Timelines and Tables

Chapter 13 contains materials that university students can use as resources in researching facts and in identifying concepts that can be linked with the themes discussed in this book.

ACKNOWLEDGMENTS

In all worthwhile endeavors, the quality of the end product is the result of discussion, encouragement, and constructive criticism. The author wishes to thank the Elementary and Early Childhood Department at Millersville University, which encouraged the development of the teaching model, and the bright, young preprofessionals whose feedback led to many refinements. The interdisciplinary projects would never have reached fruition without the advice, leadership, and support of Dr. Roger Wilson, who participated in the designing of the model.

Leo Shelly, our reference librarian, aided greatly by helping to find the elusive background material tucked away in Ganser Library. Also appreciated was the effort of Dr. Barbara Stengel, who reviewed the history section and provided valuable insights. Our appreciation goes to the following reviewers for their comments on the manuscript: Marlene Anthony, North Georgia College and State University, and Dr. Anna M. Stave, State University of New York at Oneonta.

Finally, I wish to thank our editors, Frances Helland and Norris Harrell, who eliminated all the snags along the way.

CHAPTER 1

TEN YEARS OF EDUCATIONAL REFORM

Chapter 1 discusses current trends in teaching, the political and social forces that drive these trends, and their effect on teachers and elementary school curriculum.

There is no role more important to a society than that of an educator. A country's future relies on the skills, knowledge, and products of its schooling. Schools reflect the beliefs and aspirations of a nation; therefore schooling must be responsive to the values, the social milieu, and the political climate of the period. The last decade was an era of accountability when politicians, educators, parents, and government debated the cost, value, and effectiveness of our educational system.

■ What were the factors driving educational reform?

■ How have these debates affected the role of teachers and the curriculum?

Educational Reform
Grant Funding Agencies
Parents
Policy Makers
Professional Organizations
Teachers

Curriculum
Accountability Viewpoint ■ National or State Control ■ Standardized Curriculum ■ Standardized Goals ■ Standardized Tests ■ Emphasis on Content Knowledge
Student Learning Viewpoint ■ Local School Control ■ Team Teaching ■ Interdisciplinary Instruction ■ Emphasis on Content and Process Knowledge ■ Formal and Authentic Assessment

Teacher Education
Program Accountability
Tougher Academic Standards

TEACHER EDUCATION

Cornett (1995) believed that a decade of teacher criticism and efforts to reform education began on June 16, 1980, when *Time* magazine published an article with the headline "Help, Teachers Can't Teach." This article reported the results of a national study completed the previous year that concluded that the brightest and best were not remaining in the field of teaching (Vance & Schlechty, 1982). Average SAT scores for education majors were declining; the shortage of science and mathematics teachers raised questions about national security; and the *Nation at Risk* report (National Commission on Excellence in Education, 1983) focused public attention on teacher preparation programs and efforts to standardize teacher licensing.

Teacher education programs also fell under the scrutiny of the public eye. Galambos, Cornett, and Spitler (1985) compared the transcripts of arts and science graduates with the transcripts of education graduates from southern colleges and universities. Galambos et al. concluded that teacher education programs were weak because education majors took fewer academic courses within their college majors than the arts and science graduates. Researchers stated that "Students often follow paths of least resistance and ferret out courses on weather and acoustics of musical instruments to meet the science requirements. These courses meet the letter but hardly the intent, of a broad general education background" (p. 27).

In 1986 reports from studies by the Holmes Group and the Carnegie Foundation initiated an effort to reform teacher education by calling for five-year programs. New approaches were recommended that called for tougher academic standards and program accountability. The question, it seemed, was to design teacher education curriculum that would assure that graduates had a broad content knowledge base, a rich understanding of child development, and skills in the selection, design, and implementation of developmentally appropriate methodology.

> What was the best way to prepare teachers for classrooms of the future in this dynamic, ever-changing political and social climate?

TRENDS, REFORMS, AND PRACTICES

Attention also shifted to the elementary school curriculum when a coalition of business executives, politicians, professors, and policy makers called for national educational standards. National standards had the potential of both positive and negative results. Standards could challenge students to demonstrate greater scholarship, encourage more authentic, broader based assessment, and create a demand for a more intellectually stimulating curriculum. On the other hand, they could result in a rigid, outdated curriculum geared to national tests that were inconsistent with the values and objectives of individual students and communities. In addition, they had the potential for minimizing the role of the classroom teacher.

Eisner (1991) described the White House April 18, 1991, announcement of a multidimensional plan a "lever for reform of American schools." This plan called for national examinations, a national report card, funding for model schools, and financial incentives for achievement in the core academic subjects. He claimed that none of these proposals were new, that model schools had been discussed for decades, and that national testing was introduced twenty years before in the form of the National Assessment of Educational Progress. Predicting that this proposal was the forerunner of a national curriculum, Eisner questioned the value of a national curriculum by asking how the proposed changes would enrich the educational experience and improve the service to at-risk students.

In 1987 the American public seemed to endorse a national curriculum. The Gallup Poll indicated that most Americans believed that standardized goals and standardized curriculums were desirable. In the same poll, respondents provided solid, positive ratings for local schools but were less content with schools in general.

Eisner felt this finding was understandable considering the picture of education depicted by the mass media. He stated that "the proposal to develop a national curriculum is a natural outgrowth of the public's feeling of desperation that our educational ship is sinking and that a national examination system is necessary to provide data that make it possible to interpret student performance" (p. 76).

It seemed ironic that while national standards and curricula homogenized local and regional differences by getting all students to run on the same track, there was also increased interest and acknowledgment of our nation's cultural diversity. In addition, the United States had a long tradition of state and local control of schools. States had the ultimate responsibility for education since they defined minimal educational conditions under which schools were to function.

> If the United States adopted a national curriculum, how would roles of school and teachers change? Teachers were trained professionals. Was it their responsibility to adapt curricula to meet the skill levels, attention spans, and content backgrounds of pupils, or were they technicians who executed the purposes of others?

Eisner felt that almost all of the proclamations for school reform neglected the deeper mission of schooling: the stimulation of curiosity, the cultivation of intellect, the refinement of sensibilities, the growth of imagination, and the desire to use these unique and special human potentialities. Reform to Eisner meant more than revising the current educational system. Eisner challenged educators to think beyond short-term, quick-fix solutions and address our intentions and their implications for what we actually do in the schools. In his vision of reform, attention must be devoted to the structure of the workplace, the character of the curriculum, the improvement of teaching practices, and the forms employed to appraise the quality of life we lead.

Sizer (O'Neil, 1995) agreed with Eisner's assessment of the school reform movement by stating that reforms of the 1980s "were like ordering a Model T to drive 60 miles an hour. You can order all you want, but unless you change the vehicle, right down to how the engine's organized, you're not going to go 60 miles an hour" (p. 4). He felt that too many reforms never questioned the basic assumptions of how schools were organized and the way schools were run—"They may have changed the hubcaps of the problem, but it's still a Model T" (p. 4).

Sizer believed that there was no single educational model, since every school had to reflect its own community. His research concluded that long-term success was only possible if there was powerful support and collaboration among teachers in smaller schools in which principals, teachers, students, and influential community members knew each other. Another important factor was lower pupil/teacher ratios, which Sizer felt could be accomplished by creating teams of teachers.

Sizer valued exhibitions of students' intellectual work and stated that most serious scholars felt that content subjects could not be constructively separated. Content integration was verified by the American Association for the Advancement of Science's Project 2061 which showed the necessary and powerful interconnections between chemistry, physics, biology, mathematics, and technology. Sizer viewed all education as outcome based and felt that freedom of choice should remain at local levels and include parents, teachers, principals, administrators, and the community.

Brandt (1995) wondered how educators, who appear to have very different views of measures that should be taken to improve schooling, could do a better job of communicating with the media and the public who valued safety, order, and the "basics." He suggested three options. If educators believed the public was right, they should rethink their priorities and place more emphasis on safety and order. If educators thought the public misunderstood, they must do a better job communicating their views. If educators were convinced the public was wrong, they must demonstrate leadership and do some constituency building to develop support for their practices.

By 1996 some people believed that the standards movement was dead, undermined by a change in politics and the demise of the National Educational Standards and Improvement Council (NESIC). NESIC was created as a part of the Goals 2000 legislation in 1994 and was charged with the responsibility of overseeing the development of voluntary national content standards and certifying the standards created by states. However, Marzano and Kendall (1996) did not agree that the standards issue was closed.

Marzano and Kendall felt that organizing schooling around standards was so logical that schools and districts would implement the process even without state and federal mandates. There were strong indications that reform efforts that fell through at national levels were being implemented at local levels. Marzano and Kendall identified the following four reasons as driving forces behind local reform based on educational standards: (1) the erosion of the Carnegie Unit and the common curriculum, (2) the variation in current grading practices, (3) the lack of attention to educational outputs, and (4) the implementation of similar reforms in other countries.

There appeared to be general agreement that reform was needed. However, two viewpoints emerged as to how reform could be accomplished most effectively. Student learning advocates believed in student-centered, collaborative, project-oriented instruction adapted to meet individual differences. Accountability advocates felt that standards should be applied, all students should aim for the same targets, and those who could not demonstrate mastery should be held accountable. Much debate arose concerning the standards and the groups that would set them. Political pressure was being applied by policy makers, taxpayers, professional organizations, grant funding agencies, and the media.

Could standards be written in a fair and unbiased manner? How would schools meet the needs of the students who could not demonstrate mastery? Would state or national funds be provided for remedial instruction?

INTERDISCIPLINARY CURRICULUM

Teaching Philosophies: The Great Debate

The educational reform movement that fueled discussions about national standards also created a debate among educators about the most effective reading methodology. In 1987 the National Council of Teachers of English (NCTE) released a report criticizing basal readers—the Report Card on Basal Readers (1987).

Cassidy (1987) identified these criticisms as: (1) basals provided teachers with little guidance in teaching comprehension; (2) stories in the basals tended to have less well-developed plots and conflicts than stories in literature; (3) basals emphasized rigid readability formulas; (4) editors of basals changed compound sentences to simple sentences, eliminated causal relationships, discarded important information, and simplified rich, vivid language; and (5) workbook stories were often unrelated to the basal stories, pages were cluttered, and directions were unclear. Cassidy claimed that even though basals were not perfect, publishers were responsive to these concerns and took steps to improve reading materials.

However, the NCTE report and the debates among educators comparing phonics to a literature-based approach brought about many changes in elementary reading programs. Goodman, Freeman, Murphy, and Shannon (1987) stated that at the time of the report, 80 to 90 percent of the schools taught reading through basal readers. Shortly after this statistic was printed, many schools began urging their professional staff to attend workshops to learn about the literature approach.

Whole language originated in New Zealand and was based on the assumption that children learned to read in the same way they learned to talk, by absorbing and modeling the language around them. Children in whole language classrooms listened to literature, wrote stories containing invented spellings, and predicted the meanings of words through context clues.

> The debate about reading instruction paralleled the controversy about interdisciplinary instruction. Should instruction be provided in discrete, separate units or should concepts be introduced when they were most meaningful and contributed to the solution of a problem?

By the late 1980s, many districts were implementing whole language in elementary classrooms. Emphasis was placed on creating literacy experiences for children rather than drilling phonics rules, giving paper and pencil tests, and teaching isolated grammar rules.

Advocates of whole language believed that children demonstrated understanding of phonics through invented spelling, but Jeanne Chall dismissed the "incidental" phonics observed in whole language classrooms. Commenting on the cyclical nature of the debate over instruction and achievement, Chall said, "Educators resist phonics and any kind of direct teaching. They put so much emphasis on interest and joyfulness. However, you can't say to a mother whose child can't read, 'yes, but he enjoys books' " (Jones, 1996, p. 17).

In the spring of 1995, parents, taxpayers, and politicians demanded that Governor Pete Wilson sign a back-to-the-basics law when California students scored next to the lowest on the National Assessment of Educational Progress exam. (Only

Louisiana students scored lower.) The law, known as the ABC law, required public schools to teach phonics. California's decision resulted in raising doubt again about the philosophy and techniques for teaching reading. Many educators interpreted the California legislation as a backlash against interdisciplinary instruction leading to the return of rote memorization of rules, isolated grammar drills, and workbook exercises. California was a bellwether state. Educators monitored the situation in California and wondered if this legislative action would affect decisions in other states.

> Would California's decision to require skill-based instruction and the resulting media debate cause the public in other states to question process rather than product-driven and teacher-designed curriculum?

A survey of twenty-two literacy leaders' opinions on *What's Hot, What's Not for 1997* (Cassidy & Wenrich, 1997) revealed that the majority of researchers and practitioners identified direct instruction, phonics, and skills instruction as hot topics. One hundred percent predicted that balanced reading instruction (interactive philosophy) would be hot in the coming year. The debate centered on differences in teaching philosophies.

> Instruction that draws from both philosophies provides the greatest hope for success in the future. Blending rich exposure to literature with knowledge of phonics and frequent reading and writing experiences provide children with a solid foundation in reading skills. The success of these approaches, however, depends on the expertise of our teachers, since they will become the sculptors of the curriculum in each of their classrooms.

The Integrated Curriculum: A Historical Perspective

Opinions differ about the beginning of interest in integrating school curriculum. In a doctoral dissertation, Stack (1961) traced the beginnings of the psychological and philosophical framework for the core curriculum to the 1800s through the writings of Herbert Spencer. Harville (1954) supported the interdisciplinary approach by citing early twentieth century trends in education, anthropology, and psychology. Fraley (1978) reported the work of Hollis Caswell and Harold Alberty in integrating core curriculum. Smith (1997) stated that many educators traced the rise of integrated language arts to the success of integrated curriculum in Great Britain in the 1960s and 1970s.

However, both Vars (1991a) and Smith (1997) agreed that the curriculum reform movement of the 1930s and Dewey's discussion of meaningful, student-centered learning fueled the progressive view of integrated instruction. Vars cited the research of Thaiss (1984), which revealed a close connection between language and cognition but showed that even though teachers favor an integrated approach, only minimal amounts of integration took place in most classrooms.

In his discussion of integrating language arts, Smith (1997) identified several reasons why the approach was not implemented in most schools. Many teachers

FIGURE 1.1

Teaching Philosophies

Efferent Philosophy	Interactive Philosophy	Aesthetic Philosophy
Linear teaching of skills	Emphasizes both skills and experiences	Emphasis on creating literacy experiences
Deductive instruction	Uses both inductive and deductive practices	Inductive instruction
Use of published materials	Uses published materials, reading/writing methods, and interdisciplinary instruction	Use of reading and writing methods
Emphasis on drill and practice	Uses skill practice with authentic experiences	Creates authentic reading and writing experiences
Teacher directed	Both teacher directed and student centered	Student centered
Teaches from parts to whole	Teaches both parts and whole based on purposes of instruction	Teaches from whole to parts

were not prepared to switch from a skills-based to an integrated curriculum, felt that such a move would be revolutionary, and lacked the confidence to replace their traditional instruction with new techniques.

Also, most public schools in the United States set up rigid constraints on time, curricular content, and planning. These constraints inhibited teacher collaboration and discouraged teachers' efforts to integrate subject matter. An additional inhibiting factor was the public's excessive trust in "teacher-proof" learning programs, along with the so-called objectivity of standardized tests which tended to reinforce teachers' lack of confidence in the ability to create integrated instruction.

Brazee and Capelluti (1995) lamented the fact that districts were so resistant to the idea of curriculum reform. "It's 1994 and our kids play with voice-controlled toys; we can make a phone call and see the person we're talking to; cars can give us directions to a strange city. . . . and yet, the school program is essentially the same as it was 25, even 50 years ago" (p. 3). They continue to describe prevalent school curriculums: "teachers still work in isolation from one another; the separate subject approach still dominates curriculum delivery; students are still placed in rigid tracks with varying expectations for achievement; and students are passive recipients of information" (p. 3).

Brazee and Capelluti believed that change was a highly personal experience and that schools do not change, people do. The initiative for change in the curriculum and the way it was delivered began when school personnel examined their beliefs. Without this philosophical discussion, no serious reform could take place. In their report to the National Middle School Association, Brazee and Capelluti identified four beliefs that must be affirmed before teaching practices can be reshaped.

1. All children can succeed and should be held accountable to high expectations.
2. Team work and individual effort should be rewarded.

3. Learning should be relevant and responsive to the learner at the time it occurs.
4. An integrative approach to curriculum rather than separate subject isolation makes sense.

What Is an Integrated Curriculum?

Brazee and Capelluti described an integrated curriculum as follows:

> Integrated curriculum is based on a holistic view of learning and recognizes the necessity for learners to see the big picture rather than to require learning to be divided into small pieces. Integrative curriculum ignores traditional subject lines while exploring questions that are most relevant to students. As a result, it is both responsive to students' needs and intellectual because it focuses on helping learners use their minds as well. There is in fact, no one integrative curriculum, but rather principles of teaching and learning that guide the development of integrative curriculum in diverse settings. (Brazee and Capelluti, 1995, p. 9)

Integrated curricula attempted to dissolve boundaries, to assist students in making connections between disciplines, and to help students solve problems in their own world through research and critical reasoning. Beane (1990) felt that "the separate subject curriculum is alien to life itself and just bad learning theory" (p. 21). However, the most comprehensive study that confirmed this belief was the work of Aikin (1942).

Aikin's eight year study demonstrated that graduates of thirty experimental high schools performed better on both academic and social measures than did matched peers from a traditional subject-centered program. The most dramatic finding was that graduates from the six high schools that varied the most from the separate subject curriculum model and used a variety of integrated approaches achieved higher ratings than all other students in the research project. Aikin's findings and the results of more than eighty normative or comparative studies conducted since then, such as the Bibliography of Research on the Effectiveness of Block Time, Core, and Interdisciplinary Team Teaching Programs (National Association for Core Curriculum, 1984), supported the integrated model approach.

Vars (1991b) stated that despite the solid research base demonstrating the success of integrated instruction, interest in core-type programs waxed and waned as public schools in the United States vacillated between subject matter acquisition to social problems and back again. Until recently, most intermediate and middle school curricula were traditional. During the last four years, curriculum conversations exploded. Both philosophies and practices were examined as school personnel discussed their roles in light of the new possibilities and demands brought about by curriculum reform.

This self-reflection led to the realization that there was a need to help students get the big picture and make sense of life experiences rather than acquire the bits and pieces of knowledge being taught in the typical splintered, over-departmentalized school curriculum. Curriculum integration was "in" again.

CLOSURE STATEMENT

School reform is a very political issue because it impacts the finances and quality of life of every household. While businesses are concerned about hiring a literate workforce, parents worry about their child being accepted into college, and retirees urge school districts to eliminate services to curtail taxes. In the last several decades, technology has advanced very rapidly, opening up new avenues of communication and information via the World Wide Web and the Internet. In this technological and political arena, many schools struggle to afford the equipment, train professional staff in its use, determine how technology can support existing curricula, and explain the expenditures to the community. Knowledge is expanding rapidly, and many employed workers will not have incomes in the future if they do not retrain to develop and refine new skills.

The standards movement assumes that knowledge is static and, after demonstrating mastery of a set of concepts by passing a standardized test, learners will be prepared for success in life. Unfortunately, children have different skill levels, attention spans, experiential backgrounds, and adult aspirations. To further complicate matters, the body of knowledge required for success expands routinely. Teachers must emphasize content acquisition without neglecting the learning process. The ultimate objective should be to make all children independent learners.

An integrated curriculum is flexible enough to allow students to research topics consistent with their interests and in varying levels of depth. Concepts become easier to understand when they are related to the solution of a problem. In addition, schoolwork is more interesting to the learners because content is relevant to their lives.

Skills, content, and processes must be integrated into the curriculum. The most valuable asset any school district can have as a reform agent is a well-trained, creative teacher. A teacher can observe children and modify or supplement the instruction to fit the unique talents of the children in the classroom. Today's teacher must be prepared and feel confident as a decision maker.

Interdisciplinary curriculum provides opportunities for ongoing professional growth. As teachers design instruction, their research leads to broader and broader schema and in-depth content understandings. As we observe children, read their papers, and listen to their reports, we grow as educators.

Interdisciplinary instruction is a collaborative activity. The insights of our colleagues help in making our judgments about students and their products more objective. Just as we learn from students, we also learn through our contact with colleagues. Networking is an important outgrowth of interdisciplinary instruction. Educational change comes slowly, but examination of the social forces that influence school reform explains trends in education.

We can glean ideas from other programs in other schools, but curricula must reflect the values and the aspirations of families in each community. However, it is very important for teachers, parents, politicians, and students to realize that mastery of a set of standard skills will not solve all problems or meet the needs of every learner. Ultimately, curriculum must be developed locally and teachers must be empowered to make the decisions to adapt curriculum to fit the learning styles, attention spans, and skill levels of a wide range of abilities.

Informed, talented, and creative teachers bring about educational reform through interactions with students and their families. Integrated curriculum is the key to the reform movement and teachers must be trained to use problem-solving techniques to spark the desire to learn.

REFERENCES

Aikin, W. (1942). *The story of an eight year study.* New York: Harper & Row.

Beane, J. (1990). *A middle school curriculum: From rhetoric to reality.* Columbus, OH: National Middle School Association.

Brandt, R. (1995). What does the public want? *Educational Leadership, 52*(5), 3.

Brazee, E N., & Capelluti, J. (1993). Why an integrative curriculum for middle level: A recent rationale. *NELMS Journal, 6*(3), 21–27.

Brazee, E. N., & Capelluti, J. (1995). *Dissolving boundaries: Toward an integrative curriculum.* Columbus, OH: National Middle States Association.

Cassidy, W. J. (1987). Basals are better. *Learning,* 65–66.

Cassidy, W. J., & Wenrich, J. K. (1997, February/March). What's hot, what's not for 1997. *Reading Today,* 34.

Cornett, L. M. (1995). Lessons from 10 years of teacher improvement reforms. *Educational Leadership, 52*(5), 26–30.

Cornett, L. M. & Gaines, G. (1994). *Reflecting on ten years of incentive programs.* Atlanta, GA: Southern Regional Education Board.

Eisner, E. (1991). Should America have a national curriculum? *Educational Leadership, 49*(2), 76–81.

Fraley, R. C. (1978). *Core curriculum: An epic in the history of educational reform* (Doctoral dissertation, Teachers College, Columbia University, 1978). *Dissertation Abstracts International 38,* 10: 5883A.

Galambos, E. L., Cornett, L. M., & Spitler, H. (1985). *An analysis of transcripts of teachers and arts and sciences graduates.* Atlanta, GA: Southern Regional Education Board.

Goodman, K. S., Freeman, Y., Murphy, S., & Shannon, P. (1987). *Report card on basal readers.* Columbia, MS: Commission on Reading, National Council of Teachers of English.

Harville, H. (1954). Origins of the core concept. *Social Education, 18*(4), 161–163.

Jones, R. (1996). Skirmishes on the reading front: Is it time for a truce between phonics and whole language? *The American School Board Journal,* 15–18.

Marzano, R. J., & Kendall, J. S. (1996). *The rise and fall of standards-based education. Issues in brief.* Aurora, CO: Mid-Continent Regional Educational Lab, NASBE Publications.

National Association for Core Curriculum. (1984). *Bibliography of research on the effectiveness of block time, core, and interdisciplinary team teaching programs.* Kent, OH: Author.

National Commission on Excellence in Education. (1983, April). *A nation at risk: A report to the nation.* Washington, DC: U.S. Government Printing Office.

National Council of Teachers of English. (1987, November). *Report card on basal readers.* Columbia, MS: Commission on Reading.

O'Neil, J. (1995). On lasting school reform: A conversation with Ted Sizer. *Educational Leadership, 52*(5), 4–9.

Smith, C. B. (1997). *Integrating language arts* (Report No. EDO-CS-97-01). Urbana, IL: Clearing House on Reading, English, and Communication. (ERIC Document Reproduction Service No. ED 402 629)

Stack, E. C. (1961). *The philosophical and psychological antecedents of the core curriculum in educational theory, 1800–1918* (Doctoral dissertation, University of North Carolina, 1961), *Dissertation Abstracts International 20,* 1830–1831.

Thaiss, C. (1984). *Language across the curriculum* (Report No. 400-83-0025). Urbana, IL: Clearing House on Reading, English, and Communication. (ERIC Document Reproduction Service No. ED 250 699)

Vance, V. S., & Schlechty, P. C. (1982). The distribution of academic ability in the teaching force: Policy implications. *Phi Delta Kappan, 64,* 22–27.

Vars, G. F. (1991a). Current concepts of core curriculum: Alternative designs for integrative programs. *Transescence, 19*(1), 18–21.

Vars, G. F. (1991b). Integrated curriculum in historical perspective. *Educational Leadership, 49*(2), 14–15.

CHAPTER

TEACHING FOR UNDERSTANDING AND TRANSFER: INTERDISCIPLINARY INSTRUCTION

Chapter 2 describes strategies and techniques that are consistent with the research findings on cognition and information processing. This background information guides the decisions made in the construction of the interdisciplinary unit. After reading the chapter, preservice teachers will know how practicing professionals teach and how elementary students learn.

Committing ourselves to a career in teaching carries with it a promise of a lifetime of scholarship. Every day new discoveries are made about the way children and adults process and store information. Many of these discoveries are the result of innovative teachers who carefully observe the behavior of children as they respond to instruction.

■ What did we learn about information processing during the last decade and how will this knowledge affect our classrooms?

Teaching for Understanding and Transfer: Interdisciplinary Instruction

The Components
- Generate Topics
- Identify Goals
- Identify Performances
- Make Ongoing Assessments

Curriculum Design
- Discipline-Based Design
- Parallel Disciplines
- Multidisciplinary Design
- Interdisciplinary Design
- Integrated Day Design
- Field-Based Instruction

Individual Differences
- Multiple Intelligences
  Linguistic
  Logical/Mathematical
  Spatial
  Bodily/Kinesthetic
  Musical
  Interpersonal
  Intrapersonal
  Naturalistic

Strategies
- Visual Literacy and Learning
- The Socratic Method
- Brainstorming
- Collaborative Learning
  Rationale
  Practices
  Benefits and Shortcomings
- Grouping Practices and Tasks

THE COMPONENTS

Every teacher believes that it is important to engage students in activities that stimulate critical thinking by drawing connections between students' lives and the subject matter, between principles and practices, and between the past and present. However, researchers at the Harvard Graduate School found in their Teaching for Understanding Project what educators have suspected for some time: teachers felt that students were not understanding concepts.

Even though instructors looked for opportunities to clarify content, explained ideas clearly, and provided open-ended tasks, they were still dissatisfied with students' understanding of subject matter. The study concluded that teaching for understanding was just one of the many objectives that demanded teachers' attention; school assessments often did not support and were not consistent with this type of learning; and little information was available about the most effective strategies for teaching (Perkins & Blythe, 1994).

To know a concept in depth and to demonstrate understanding, a student must be able to explain the topic, find evidence and examples, and generalize, apply, and relate the information to a new situation. To paraphrase a concept is not enough; students must carry out tasks that show understanding and, at the same time, use the information in a new and creative way.

Perkins and Blythe believe that while experiences can be varied, many routine classroom activities do not provide stimulation that expands learning beyond what students already know. True–false quizzes, arithmetic drills, and spelling games have a place, but they do not build understanding. We learn more quickly and retain knowledge longer if it has meaning in our lives. Applying new information to a variety of contexts results in a comfort level that helps learners to feel ownership of the concepts studied.

To create a curriculum and a classroom that values and implements understanding, Perkins and Blythe recommend the following framework. The framework can be used in discussing or planning a unit, a topic, or a course.

1. *Generate Topics.* The selection of a topic (theme, theory, historical period, and so forth) is an important decision since all topics do not lend themselves equally to teaching for understanding. A generative topic should be selected on the basis of three variables.
   a. Centrality to the discipline
   b. Accessibility to the students
   c. Conceivability to diverse topics inside and outside the discipline
2. *Identify Goals.* Because topics can be very broad, teachers need to focus projects by identifying goals that become the targets to be met.
3. *Identify Performances.* After providing focus through the goals, teachers need to identify performances that lead to the development of deep understanding from the beginning to the end of the unit.
4. *Make Ongoing Assessments.* Traditional assessment occurs at the end of a project and focuses on grading and accountability. Learning for understanding requires a criteria, opportunities for reflection and revision, and feedback. Feedback can be provided by teachers, parents, and peers, or it can consist of self-evaluation (Perkins & Blythe, 1994).

The authors identified these four instructional factors as guidelines for developing a curriculum that fosters teaching for understanding. However, they are quick to admit that other variables such as classroom structure and student–teacher relationships also contribute to successful implementation.

Because curriculum integration is a cooperative activity that involves administrators, supervisors, and teachers, communication, cooperation, support, and careful planning are vital elements. Decisions must take into account the values, aspirations, and interests of the students; the philosophy of the school district; the state and discipline benchmarks; availability of materials; budgetary allowances; and time limitations imposed by the school schedule.

CURRICULUM DESIGN

Jacobs (1989) contends that teachers must be active curriculum designers and make the decisions concerning the nature and degree of integration and the scope and sequence of the content. Her six curriculum options differ by the amount of planning and implementation time, student–teacher empowerment, and subject matter focus. Descriptions of the six curriculum options follow.

Discipline-Based Design

In this traditional design, subjects are taught in separate time blocks throughout the school day and no attempt is made to integrate. Knowledge is presented in separate fields without a deliberate attempt to show relationships among them. This approach is often used when introducing new material or developing a knowledge base.

Parallel Disciplines

In the parallel design, teachers meet and sequence lessons so that topics in two related disciplines are taught during the same time frame. The content and the presentations are not restructured, and it is the responsibility of the students to see the relationship between subject areas. (A history teacher covers the revolutionary period while the English teacher assigns students to read *Johnny Tremain*). This design is rarely monitored during implementation and takes relatively little initial planning.

Multidisciplinary Design

The multidisciplinary option brings together related disciplines in a formal unit or course structured around a common theme. It is different from the parallel design in which teachers follow a prescribed subject matter scope and sequence without modifying presentations. In the multidisciplinary approach, teachers meet initially, select a theme, and modify content presentations to fit the theme selected. Teachers must have a common planning period to make curriculum decisions and outline content.

Interdisciplinary Design

In this design, periodic units or courses of study deliberately bring together the full range of disciplines in the school's curriculum. Curriculum designers meet in common planning periods as they plan, monitor, modify, and evaluate instruction related to a common theme. The units are of specific duration and are planned to meet a mutually agreed on set of common understandings.

Integrated Day Design

This model is based on issues or topics that emerge from the child's world or curiosity. It involves making the most of a teachable moment. A teacher may have very little preparation for this activity or unit of study and must be knowledgeable if it is to be effective. Students are empowered in this model because it is driven by their interests, skills, and experiential backgrounds.

Field-Based Instruction

This is the most extreme form of interdisciplinary work. Students live in the school environment and create the curriculum out of their day-to-day lives. Students who are interested in buildings might research, compare, and contrast school architecture with architecture developed in other periods. This is a totally integrated program because the student's life is synonymous with the school.

Jacobs urges educators to use the full range of curriculum options when designing instruction. Decisions should be based on limitations or level of support established by the school structure, characteristics of the students, community values, and content.

INDIVIDUAL DIFFERENCES

Multiple Intelligences

In 1983 Howard Gardner published *Frames of the Mind,* which introduced a pluralistic view of intelligence that contrasted sharply with Binet's scales, which produced a single score. Gardner's view suggested that human intelligence entailed a set of skills that enabled individuals to solve problems, create products, and formulate new problems in a context-rich, naturalistic setting.

Binet's intelligence scales were developed to identify children who were having difficulty in school tasks and might benefit from special education. Though he never intended to attribute intelligence to a single trait, the fact that his test results were reported in a single score reinforced this belief.

Gardner did not rely on psychometric findings in formulating his theory, but conducted research in human development and neurology. For years, Gardner studied normal and special individuals including autistic children, prodigies, idiot savants, and brain damaged patients. His work at Boston University School of Medicine, the Veterans Administration Medical Center of Boston, and Harvard's Project Zero were combined with observations of cultures around the world and used to formulate the multiple intelligences theory. Key points in Gardner's theory follow.

1. All definitions of intelligence are shaped by time, place, and culture.
2. Intelligence is galvanized by participation in some kind of culturally valued activity and the individual's growth follows a developmental path.
3. The eight intelligences are:

Linguistic	The capacity to use words effectively
Logical/Mathematical	The capacity to use numbers effectively
Spatial	The ability to perceive the visual spatial world accurately
Bodily/Kinesthetic	Expertise in using one's body to express ideas and feelings

Musical	The capacity to perceive, discriminate, transform, and express musical forms
Interpersonal	The ability to perceive and make distinctions in the moods, intentions, motivations, and feelings of others
Intrapersonal	Self-knowledge and the ability to act adaptively on the basis of that knowledge
Naturalistic	The ability to discriminate among living things and sensitivity to features of the natural world

4. Each person has all eight intelligences.
5. Most people develop each intelligence to an adequate level of competency.
6. Intelligences work together in complex ways.
7. There are many ways to be intelligent within each category.
8. Development depends on biological endowment, cultural and historical development, and personal life history.
9. Crystallizing experiences cause turning points.

Gardner (1997) states that while all human beings have all intelligences, they do not have the same strengths in each area. Just as we have different personalities, we have different minds. Gardner urges teachers to take students' individual differences very seriously and gear both curriculum and assessment to students' minds. He reminds teachers that the multiple intelligences theory was not based on school work or tests, but from the world and those things that are valued in the world.

> If an activity is not related to something that is valued in the world, the school has probably lost the core idea of multiple intelligences, which is that these intelligences evolved to help people do things that really matter in the real world. . . . The theory in and of itself, is not going to solve anything in society, but linking multiple intelligences with curriculum focused on understanding is an extremely powerful intellectual undertaking. (p. 11)

STRATEGIES

> In our rush to lead children into critical thinking activities, we sometimes forget that children cannot successfully perform critical thinking tasks if they do not have the knowledge base. It is not enough to create a learning environment; students must be taught how to use the environment and the information observed through experiences to solve problems. What can teachers do to help children become more observant and apply the information they have observed?

Visual Literacy and Learning

The ability to use imagery in many ways—for remembering, for manipulation, and for transformation—enhances students' ability to learn. Some people go on a walk and see nothing. Others see little. A few people see a lot because they have learned to observe and reflect, to concentrate on an object, and to elaborate mentally through imagery (Seels & Dunn, 1989). Visual literacy can be defined as the ability to receive, process, relate to past experiences, and respond to the pictures one sees.

Print is all around us in advertisements, illustrations, and television; however, schools provide very little instruction in visual literacy. Goldstone (1989) feels that the neglect of visual literacy is related to the assumption that it is a natural aspect of cognitive development, is built into the cognitive structure, and is analogous to learning to speak. She alerts educators that "children come to school with the ability to interpret on a literal level and perceive images as a whole. However, the higher-order thinking skills of analyzing, synthesizing, and interpreting the visual image do not come naturally" (p. 592).

Interpreting visual images is a higher-order activity requiring the student to use abstract thinking skills. Goldstone believes that there is a link between creating mental images from a text and the ability to acquire literacy. "When the capacity for interpreting images is weak, comprehension is at best superficial. Without imagery, depth of meaning and richness of style is lost" (p. 593).

Sinatra, Beaudry, Stahl-Gemake, and Guastello (1990) recommend the use of visual and text strategies to improve the comprehension and writing skills of students who do not have the background experience to understand content and who are unable to organize their writing due to a lack of form and sentence sense. There are three components of visual learning: input strategies, output strategies, and integrative strategies.

Input occurs when a teacher uses a picture or a film to stimulate thinking. Information is taken in through the eyes and is processed in the brain where it is converted into meaning. Output results when the child has an idea that is used to create a poem, a picture, or a composition. The idea is converted into a tangible product that is an outward expression of the child's thoughts. In the integrative process, the child has an idea that is categorized or organized in a visual form that stimulates additional thought or ideas. This is by far the most powerful strategy and is used most frequently by teachers in the form of a chart, a web, or a graphic organizer.

Visual interpretations begin with the concrete and progress into more abstract thinking processes. Children who are trained to observe and interpret concrete images develop the ability and the confidence to master a more symbolic form—such as print. In written text, children are required to interpret graphic symbols. Experiences with visual literacy tasks train students in the behaviors, attitudes, and questions that are so important in thinking abstractly and analytically (Goldstone, 1989).

Comprehension is an interaction between the author and the reader. Literacy occurs when the reader brings experiences to the printed page and moves beyond literal decoding to a more abstract level that involves interpretation of the message. The teaching of visual literacy is not just a scaffolding technique but an integral part of the communication process that protects readers from the influence of propaganda and encourages independent, creative thinking. Graphic organizers order information and show relationships. Once information becomes meaningful, it is much easier to remember.

The Socratic Method: Questioning and Problem Solving

As technology advances, there appears to be little debate about the type of reasoning employers will require of their employees. More and more studies show that employers want employees who can reason, solve problems, and make decisions.

Brown (1991) found that even though these attributes were valued by educators, students in U.S. public schools were not receiving instruction that fostered critical thinking or developing the ability to make reasoned decisions.

Lambright (1995) contends that there was a recognition that critical thinking skills were absolutely required and that big changes were needed. However, she believes that reform requires internal change and personal effort and is doomed to failure if mandated by outside authority. The ability to reason comes from inside ourselves because it must involve a change in attitude if it is to make a long-lasting impact.

Lambright feels that Gray's (1989) Socratic seminars provide the vehicle for true reform and a break from rote instruction leading to conformity. Gray categorized instruction into three groupings:

1. *Coaching.* Instruction in reading, writing, and math computation.
2. *Didactic lectures.* Deductive presentations of content.
3. *Socratic seminar.* A question and discussion process where students examine the content they have learned to analyze problems, hypothesize solutions, and draw conclusions.

The Socratic seminars were stimulating intellectual conversations focused on a reading that could be an essay, a poem, a technical report, an artifact, a painting, or a video. The facilitator prepared the experience by selecting a challenging reading, analyzing the text for literal and deeper meaning, and identifying the ideas, values, and issues raised by the content.

The last part of the preparation involved developing a broad opening question that connected the text with the audience of readers. Skill in formulating questions made the difference between success and failure, so curriculum developers continually strove to challenge readers by raising issues that piqued curiosity and encouraged debate. "If Benjamin Franklin and Thomas Jefferson lived today, how would their beliefs agree or conflict with current views on immigration and women's rights?" "Is there a relationship between women's clothing and society's view of their role in the family and the workplace?" The questions challenged students to form an opinion that had to be supported by published data.

Tredway (1995) contended that even though Socratic seminars were introduced in the schools in the 1980s as a reform initiative to develop critical thinking skills and evidenced success, Socratic seminars were conspicuously absent in most classrooms today. In the seminars (usually taught in a 50–80 minute period once a week), students discussed the question related to their reading, thought deeply about the issue, looked at ethical issues, cited opinions, supported their ideas with documentation, and reacted to the ideas of others.

Lambright (1995) observed that the process required the facilitator to give up control, embrace thoughtfulness, listen closely, speak carefully, and delve beneath the surface so that students learned to analyze the implications of their decisions. The preparation, the actual seminar, and the feedback period formed a gestalt that kindled higher-order learning. Students were actively and cooperatively engaged in forming ethical attitudes and behaviors with material and issues that were relevant to their lives.

In addition, they learned social and metacognitive skills. Students learned to paraphrase, defer, and take turns, as well as deal with frustration while waiting. They did not raise their hands, but used body language, eye contact, and mutual respect to follow the seminar process (Tredway, 1995).

This type of active learning is helpful to teachers as well as students. When students discuss their opinions, teachers listen carefully for any gaps in understanding. The discussions provide opportunities for ongoing assessment and set purposes for additional research, reteaching of skills, or content-centered mini-lessons.

Brainstorming: Stimulating Reasoning

Every student comes to the classroom with background experiences and preconceived mind sets. These cultural, psychological, and perceptual biases can interfere with problem solving by limiting one's view of alternative solutions. Since most classrooms are made up of children who have very diverse past experiences, brainstorming can be a useful technique for helping students see a problem from a new and creative perspective.

The first step in the brainstorming process is *awareness and curiosity*. Before a subject or problem can be discussed logically, there must be some background understanding and a desire to investigate possible solutions. It is also important that learners demonstrate *confidence and perseverance*. Students who are not good critical thinkers assume that decisions are made through instinct. Good critical thinkers weigh information, try solutions, reject invalid data, look for alternative answers, and justify conclusions. Problem solving involves risk-taking, openness to new ideas, and reserving judgment until all options have been explored. Students who do not feel confident about their abilities may give up on a problem when they are very close to the solution. Group work and oral modeling contribute to helping students view themselves as successful problem solvers.

Cognitive dissonance occurs when a concept does not fit with our mind sets. When this happens, we can reject the new information as a mistake or try to validate the information and change our old beliefs. Though we all have a tendency to reject information that does not agree with our beliefs, remember that most discoveries and inventions occurred when the explorer or inventor continued to examine reasons why information did not appear to be consistent. If Christopher Columbus had not had faith in his belief that the world was round, the course of history would be quite different.

Lateral thinking involves looking at an issue from many points of view. Creative solutions often come through trial and error. Lateral thinking enables us to look at a problem from different angles, try alternative solutions, and select the one that is best. Children need to be encouraged to think about "What would happen if . . . ?"

All of these thinking skills are developed and strengthened through brainstorming. The objective of brainstorming is to help a group of students generate a quantity of ideas in a short amount of time so they can be examined individually as possible solutions. The teacher introduces a carefully selected, open-ended question and records students' responses. After the list of responses is complete, each response is examined and rationales are discussed in light of the most appropriate solution to the question. Teaching suggestions for this activity follow.

1. *Accept all responses.*   Defer judgment until all responses have been recorded. One of the most valuable outcomes of this activity is for students to make judgments about the value of their own responses.
2. *Have students discuss rationales for their suggestions.*   A response that may seem totally inappropriate might end up being the most creative when the rationale is expressed. Also, a valuable objective of brainstorming is to model

the reasoning process. Students who are not good reasoners have a better understanding of critical thinking when it is done as a group activity and they can observe the thinking processes of classmates.

3. *Encourage quantity.* The more ideas the better because the value of the task is to evaluate and rank responses.

4. *Build understanding and synthesize suggestions.* During the evaluation stage, condense, combine, edit, and refine suggestions. Ideas do not belong to any single class member, so students should be encouraged to build upon classmates' suggestions.

Brainstorming is an excellent way to model the reasoning process. It helps students to develop skills and confidence in their ability to solve problems. All students should be encouraged to participate and teachers should listen closely to the rationales supporting or rejecting information. Discrepancies in understandings can become the topics of new investigations.

Teachers need to use judgment in designing instruction that provides opportunities for collaboration, individual work, and time for reflection. Students will be more interested in participating in activities that offer a variety of configurations and opportunities to work with different combinations of classmates.

Collaborative Learning

Rationale

The ability to work with others is a skill developed very early in life that is crucial to success. There are few occupations that do not require collaboration with others.

Employers have become very vocal about their expectations for the schools. It is not enough for employees to follow directions; the employee of the future must be able to interact well with others, process information, and solve problems. Figure 2.1 shows what employers are demanding from prospective employees.

FIGURE 2.1

What Employers Want for Teens: 1980s U.S. Department of Labor, Employment, and Training Administration Research Report

1. Learning to learn skills

2. Listening and oral communication

3. Adaptability: creative thinking and problem solving, especially in response to barriers and obstacles

4. Personal management: self-esteem, goal setting and self-motivation, personal career development and goals, pride in work accomplished

5. Group effectiveness: interpersonal skills, negotiation, teamwork

6. Organizational effectiveness and leadership: making a contribution

7. Competence in reading, writing, and computation*

*The report notes that the seventh skill, while essential, is no longer sufficient for workplace competence.

Practices

Elias et al. (1997) believe that having students work in well-structured cooperative formats helps to develop skills that are particularly important in today's and the future's team-oriented work environment. However, if cooperative learning is to be successful, several social and emotional skills must be in place. The authors state that social and emotional education results in active learning, generalization of skills across settings, and the development of decision-making and problem-solving abilities (p. 2).

Cooperative learning requires participants to demonstrate self-control, assume role-taking, and have adequate communication skills. If students are well prepared and the instruction is developmentally appropriate, both academic and social growth can be achieved.

Benefits and Shortcomings

Disagreements can occur in groups due to differences in work habits, power issues, and conflicting viewpoints. Some of these conflicts can be avoided if the instructor provides clear, well-planned instructions, limits the size of groups, and recommends specific roles for group members. We have found that odd-numbered groups of three or five work best because participants are more likely to negotiate differences of opinion.

Insecure students feel more comfortable sharing opinions with classmates in small groups. Once shared, ideas can be modified and verified before being presented to the class. Grouping students in dyads or triads is useful in building confidence and trust.

Cooperative learning encourages sharing of ideas, provides modeling of learning processes, and develops student bonding. Through participation, students learn how to listen actively, integrate the opinions of others into their views, practice negotiation and persuasion, and draw logical conclusions.

Grouping Practices and Tasks

All work should not be done in groups. Teachers need to use judgment in designing instruction that provides opportunities for collaboration, individual work, and reflection. Students will be more interested in participating in activities that offer a variety of configurations and the opportunity to work with different combinations of classmates. When roles are assigned within groups, it is important that responsibilities are rotated to allow each student a turn in each role. Figure 2.2 provides examples of grouping configurations.

FIGURE 2.2

Grouping Configurations

Group	Task
Computer Groups	Keyboard operator, observer, and editor work together on the completion of a product.
Review Buddies	Working in pairs, students provide practice of words or concepts written on notecards.
Editing Partners	One student reads a composition. A small group of classmates listen to the composition and make suggestions for revision.

FIGURE 2.2

(continued)

Group	Task
Group Reports	After assignment of a topic, students brainstorm a series of questions related to the topic, assume responsibility for researching the answers to their questions, and design a reporting format.
Group Retellings	Students gather information from different sources relating to a common topic. Information is shared with the group and integrated into class presentation.
Metacognitive Pairs	Students take turns reading a selection orally. As one student reads, the other checks for accuracy and interprets the information.
Playwrights	Using information read, students assume roles of storyboard editor, playwrights, costume designers, set designers, director, and actors.
Paired Response Groups	After hearing a book or composition read orally, listeners turn to a partner and share an idea they enjoyed or one question they would like to ask the author.
Think Aloud	After the presentation of a mini-lesson, the teacher models the thinking process (Davey, 1983).
Dyads	Working in pairs, students read two pages of text orally in unison or silently individually. The recaller paraphrases the content and the classifier listens and edits the information recalled.
Focus Trios	Working in groups of three, students summarize what they already know about the content from a reading and develop questions to answer during reading. After reading, students discuss the answers to their questions, clarify content, and summarize answers.
Jigsaw	In groups, students read different parts of the same selection. After reading, each student shares what he or she has read. Members of the group ask questions, clarify concepts, correct misunderstandings through rereading, and integrate the information (Aaronson & Goode, 1980).
Reading Buddies	Students in upper grades serve as teachers or readers for emergent readers. Readers can use a Directed Reading Activity or a Directed Reading Thinking Activity format as a framework for the lesson to be shared.
Problem Solving and Project Groups	Students work collaboratively in small groups on a research project of their choice. Through consensus, they identify a major problem to resolve, sources of information to be examined, and the format of the final product.
Test Coaches	Small groups of students each review a chapter of a text, identify the major ideas, order the concepts on a graphic organizer, develop three broad questions linking the concepts, share the graphic organizer with the class, and ask the focus questions.
Strategy Teachers and Concept Clarifiers	Working in teams, students practice metacognitive strategies of prediction, drawing inferences, and generating rationales for their opinions.

CLOSURE STATEMENT

In the 1980s technology advanced rapidly and educational institutions had to reexamine their objectives, procedures, and outcomes. Business leaders did not want employees trained to follow directions only; instead, they called for educational programs that required students to assess data, hypothesize solutions, and solve problems. Technology would not decrease literacy levels. In the future, as more and more information would become available, the ability to sort and validate data would become imperative. This task would require critical thinking.

Educators could no longer afford to teach isolated skills. Students needed to learn how to work with others on common projects that involved observing details, summarizing data, brainstorming possible solutions, asking probing questions, and evaluating responses. Researchers recommended strategies and curriculum designs while psychologists researched brain functions and learning.

Teachers were an integral part of these advances. If they were to become the crafters of the instruction, opportunities had to be provided for planning. Designing a curriculum was a creative process that involved collaborating, gathering materials, weighing the value of the materials collected, and converting them into meaningful activities linked through concepts. Research findings in the late 1980s supported curricula that fostered critical thinking through discussion, collaboration, and problem solving. All of these methods supported the philosophy and the methods that linked curriculum subjects.

REFERENCES

Aaronson, E., & Goode, E. (1980). Training teachers to implement jigsaw learning: A manual for teachers. In S. Sharan, P. Hare, C. D. Webb, & R. Hertz-Lazarowitz (Eds.), *Cooperation in education* (pp. 47–81). Provo, UT: Brigham University Press.

Binet, A., & Simon, T. (1905). Methodes nouvelles pour le diagnostique du niveaux intellectuel des anormaux [New methods for the diagnosis of the intellectual level of the abnormal]. *L'annee Psychologique, 11,* 236–245.

Brown, R. (1991). *Schools of thought.* San Francisco: Jossey-Bass.

Davey, B. (1983). Think-aloud-modeling: The cognitive processes of reading comprehension. *Journal of Reading, 27,* 44–47.

Elias, M. J., Zins, J. E., Weissberg, R. P., Frey, K. S., Greenberg, M. T., Haynes, N. M., Kessler, R., Schwab-Stone, M. E., & Shiver, T. P. (1997). *Promoting social and emotional learning.* Alexandria, VA: Association for Supervision and Curriculum Development.

Gardner, H. (1983). *Frames of the mind: The theory of multiple intelligences.* New York: Basic Books.

Gardner, H. (1997). The first seven . . . and the eighth. *Educational Leadership, 55*(1), 8–13.

Goldstone, B. P. (1989). Visual interpretation of children's books. *Reading Teacher, 42,* 592–595.

Gray, D. (1989). Putting our minds to work: How to use the seminar approach in the classroom. *American Educator, 13*(3), 16–23.

Jacobs, H. H. (Ed.). (1989). *Interdisciplinary curriculum: Design and implementation.* Alexandria, VA: Association for Supervision and Curriculum Development.

Lambright, L. L. (1995). Creating a dialogue: Socratic seminars and educational reform. *Community College Journal, 65*(4), 30–34.

Leu, D. J., & Kinzer, C. K. (1999). *Effective literacy instruction.* Upper Saddle River, NJ: Merrill.

Perkins, D., & Blythe, T. (1994). Putting understanding up front. *Educational Leadership, 51*(5), 4–7.

Seels, B., & Dunn, J. (1989). A visual literacy walk using the natural learning environment. *Tech Trends, 34,* 26–29.

Sinatra, R., Beaudry, J. S., Stahl-Gemake, J., & Guastello, E. F. (1990). Combining visual literacy, text understanding, and writing for culturally diverse students. *Journal of Reading, 33,* 612–617.

Tredway, L. (1995). Socratic seminars: Engaging students in intellectual discourse. *Educational Leadership, 53*(1), 26–29.

CHAPTER

3

SELECTING A THEME: INTRODUCING THE UNIT PROTOTYPE

Chapter 3 identifies the characteristics of a good theme, discusses the steps in planning a theme, and models the selection of a theme for an interdisciplinary unit of study on *Women of Achievement: 1860–1920*. A reading selection, *The Proper Victorian Lady,* provides background information about the topic. In the example, preservice teachers assume the role of the curriculum developers of a unit focusing on Amelia Earhart as their research subject.

Classroom teachers make more curricular decisions than any other educators or policy makers. While obviously not free to teach anything they want, teachers make final decisions about what to teach, how to teach it, and how much to introduce in discrete intervals. These decisions are a serious professional responsibility that can make the difference between student success and failure. The more a teacher knows about how to shape curricula, the more likely the decisions made will result in student achievement.

■ How do successful teachers design creative, challenging instruction?

Selecting a Theme: Introducing the Unit Prototype

Organizational Considerations
- Importance of a Theme
- Project Planning
- Characteristics of a Good Theme

Unit Prototype—American Women of Achievement: 1860–1920
- Relevance of the Theme to Teachers
- Unit Planning Procedures and Guidesheets
- Historical Background: The Proper Victorian Lady
- Historical Background: Timeline of Women's Rights 1860–1920
- Unit Plan Grading Criteria
- Unit Plan Guidesheet
- Grouping Guidelines
- Research Topics Sign-Up Sheet
- Unit Resources

ORGANIZATIONAL CONSIDERATIONS

Importance of a Theme

Educational goals and curriculum materials are created by many people on many levels. Guidelines are published by state departments of education, professional organizations, and by school boards. Curriculum materials are created by curriculum committees, curriculum specialists, and textbook publishers. All these documents and educators are important influences on the decisions teachers must make about what should be taught. Materials generated from these groups include educational outcomes, school philosophies, grade-level instructional goals, scope and sequence charts, and even specific units and lesson plans. Both the continuing dialogue and the actual materials resulting from this work have a huge influence on what is taught in the classroom. The diversity and the large number of groups involved in producing educational goals indicate just how important the curriculum development process is.

Project Planning

Creating an interdisciplinary unit is similar to sculpting a work of art from marble. It requires tools, knowledge, skills, persistence, and the right raw materials. The raw material is the content base of facts that relate to the major theme or topic of the unit. Both teachers and students can contribute to the fact finding process, but a wise teacher will have a clear understanding of the content areas to be explored in the initial stages of the project.

Knowledge about creating curriculum comes from collaborating with colleagues, developing units, and observing students as they interact with one another and with the materials. At the completion of a unit, the skillful teacher reflects on the strong and weak points of the instruction and makes notes for revisions to be implemented the next time the unit is introduced.

Skill comes with practice. Each time a unit is developed, we learn more about our students, the curriculum, and the content. Through research and fact finding, we explore new content, develop more community resources, learn uses of new technology, and expand our reserve of teaching materials.

The tools for interdisciplinary instruction are our resources—the Internet, the libraries, the books, the project guidesheets, and the guest speakers that stimulate interest in the project and provide the raw materials during the planning and implementation stages.

To become a skillful curriculum designer, you must provide the persistence in following the project to completion. It involves mixing the raw materials of content with the complex ways students learn and sculpting the material into a finished product of educational art. After you gather the content information, you will cut, carve, chisel, and chip the information into a rough shape. When the unit is actually used, you will sand off the rough edges and polish what is left into a teacher's work of art.

Like all complex human activities, being a skilled sculptor of curricula is part knowledge, part judgment, part creativity, and part trial and error. Even though you have established a clear goal, the product is likely to be shaped by the journey. Creating a curriculum is an exciting undertaking that requires thinking, planning, adapting, and modifying ideas. However, the rewards are great (Wilson, personal communication, 1997).

Characteristics of a Good Theme

The selection of a theme is an important decision that should reflect the plans and objectives for the individual students taught during the school year. A good beginning is to examine the table of contents in each of the texts the school district has selected for use in the classroom and grade level. It is useful to develop a chart of annual goals listing the skills, content, and processes that are to be included in the instruction for the coming year. Figure 3.1 illustrates such annual goals.

Once gathered, this information can be used as a checklist to ensure that the instruction is consistent with state and district requirements. In addition to helping to focus on major curriculum outcomes, the chart is also useful in explaining to parents the relationship between the unit topic and the skills and content coverage.

Education majors sometimes ask when it is appropriate to use interdisciplinary instruction with elementary students. Teachers must be familiar with the skill levels, attention spans, and interests of their students to make that decision. If students are to gather information from the library, they must have the independent reading skills to be able to accomplish this task. However, it is also possible to read information orally and have children complete follow-up activities that require application of the information to the solution of a problem. The key is to plan projects that are consistent with the academic levels of the students first in a supportive and then in an independent experience. The teacher should gradually wean students from support; that is, teacher and students should first do a project together, then students should do a project in groups, then each student should do a task independently.

Themes can be based on a common text, a scientific concept, or a problem to be solved. Because the theme will be the springboard for a variety of research projects and activities, it must contain enough depth to challenge students to find information that was previously unknown while being interesting enough to pique their curiosity. Much of the success of the unit will depend on the teacher's ability

FIGURE 3.1

Annual Goals

Skills	Content	Processes
Comprehension of biographies	1800–1920 history	Library research
Competency with electronic media	1800–1920 technology and inventions	Oral reporting
Paraphrasing written material	Use of numbers in equivalent forms	Summarizing and abstracting

FIGURE 3.2

Two Basic Designs for Interdisciplinary Instruction

Design	Process	Example
All students read the same core text.	Assignments within groups are differentiated.	Students read *Number the Stars.*
		Group 1 plots the route of Ellen's escape.
		Group 2 interviews a serviceman serving during World War II.
		Group 3 writes a play about the plot.
		Group 4 researches other heroes of World War II and shares information with the class.
Groups of students read different core texts relating to the theme.	Each group of students reads a different biography of an individual living in the period from 1860–1920 and completes the same set of assignments relating to their research subject.	Students research the story setting during the lifetime of their subject and compare it to the setting today.
		Students research the contributions of their subject and describe how they affect life today.
		Students describe how their subject overcame a problem that interfered with his/her achievements.

to develop guidesheets and supportive materials that lead students into finding, synthesizing, and accurately reporting relevant information. Figure 3.2 illustrates two basic designs with examples for interdisciplinary instruction.

UNIT PLANNING MODELED
AFTER THE UNIT PROTOTYPE

Because we believe that learning is achieved most quickly through experience, we suggest that preservice teachers work cooperatively with peers while constructing an interdisciplinary unit involving researching one subject within a core topic. The prototype topic, *American Women of Achievement,* is used to demonstrate the unit-designing process with Amelia Earhart as the research focus. The education major should assume that he or she is one of a group of five students selecting Amelia Earhart as the subject of the unit to be developed. This topic is used to model the curriculum development process. Examples of guided reading assignments, rubrics, and sample guidesheets are included as prompts to encourage the creation of materials for the project. Preservice teachers will model the multitextual design by constructing and exhibiting curriculum appropriate for elementary (fourth, fifth, and sixth graders) and middle school students. Biographical material can be researched from a variety of sources, but we have found the Chelsea House *Women of Achievement* series an excellent resource for this project.

You are ready now to become sculptors of the curriculum. The task is broken down into a series of activities that you will complete with the help of a small group of classmates. The project is set in the United States between 1860 and 1920. It is an interesting time frame to examine because many technological advances occurred and these changes affected the roles of males and females within families, educational opportunities, occupations, and values and status within the culture.

The historical background provides depth for a project designed to explore the lives of women who rose to leadership in a period when most females were expected to conform to Victorian values of behavior. In shattering this confining role, the American women of achievement experienced many hardships, but opened new opportunities and choices for the women who followed.

Relevance of the Theme to Teachers

The topic of leadership is a worthwhile project for education majors because it provides the opportunity to compare the values, culture, expectations, and achievements of females of the past with those of the present. It also gives insight into those factors that stimulate creativity, risk taking, and persistence in achieving a difficult career aspiration. Through the lives of women of achievement, prospective teachers are able to gain insight into characteristics of leadership and reflect on the events in the home, school, and community that cause individuals to challenge stereotypes and traditions.

HISTORICAL BACKGROUND

THE PROPER VICTORIAN LADY

The adult role that the Victorian middle-class girl was supposed to be preparing for was that of wife and mother. It was believed that preparation for the role should begin in childhood. While mothers were advised that the difference between boys and girls should be minimized in childhood, even during those years girls were to learn to be "little housewives." They could be physically active but it was assumed that they would play with dolls. After puberty, a Victorian girl was expected to give up both vigorous physical activity and play. When she put her hair up and donned long skirts, she was to begin preparing herself with seriousness for adult femininity.

In the early and mid-Victorian years, literature of advice directed at adolescent girls was emphatically explicit about one central feature of this adult role: accepting limits and restraints and recognizing male superiority. In the words of Sara Stickney Ellis, author of *The Daughters of England,* one of the most popular early-Victorian manuals of advice for middle-class girls, "As women, then, the first thing of importance is to be content to be inferior to men—inferior in mental power, in the same proportion as you are inferior in bodily strength" (Ellis, 1843).

In adolescence, the testing ground for adulthood, girls were to accept that they must keep a tight rein both on their aspirations and their behavior. Whereas adolescent boys were encouraged to develop independence, girls were encouraged to accept dependence on the male as a natural and inevitable part of the feminine condition. Woman is so formed as to be dependent on man. The woman who is considered the most fortunate in life has never been independent, having been transferred from the care and authority of her parents to that of her husband (Tilt, 1852).

As one writer put it, "In a happy family where both mother and father were alive and the father had achieved worldly success, the father had the right to expect smiling faces, cheerful voices, and a quietly happy welcome which falls like a balm on his harassed spirit when he comes home from the outside world." Within the household, his daughters should be "sunbeams that make everything glad," creatures whose self-forgetfulness, whose willingness to help others, would create a harmonious environment.

Girls were to be reared for domesticity, and prepared in adolescence for a dependent and subordinate position in relation to males. But the domestic role that the Victorian middle-class girl was told she must prepare for was multifaceted. [It was not the simple domesticity of the thrifty yeoman's wife, skilled only in housewifery, that was held up as a model, but the complex role of Angel in the House.] In addition to skills of housewifery, she was told that she should prepare herself to bring both aesthetic and intellectual qualities to the role of wife and mother.

Even in the early and mid-Victorian decades, it was acknowledged that a girl would need some education if she were to provide her future home with the refinements of intellectual culture. But Victorian advice books took pains to emphasize to girls that they should always keep in mind the ultimate purpose of education: to make them pleasant and useful companions to men and responsible mothers to their children. In order to achieve this goal, girls were told that their attitude toward their studies was as important as anything else they might learn.

A responsible, feminine girl, said the advice books, would neither be frivolous nor overserious about her studies. In the same way she was told to be responsible for her health, a middle-class girl was told to be responsible for her studies. In respect to her health, she was neither to ignore the inevitable fragility that was thought to accompany puberty, nor to indulge that weakness. In respect to her studies, she was told to apply herself diligently during instruction at home or at school.

After the formal instruction was over, a girl's responsibilities became even greater. Throughout the Victorian period, manuals of advice and articles in girl's magazines impressed on their readers that a daughter at home should devote a portion of each day to private study. A girl should not regard her education finished when her formal lessons came to an end; instead, she should realize that she now had a responsibility for self-education. How self-education is to be taken up and how to divide the time left for intellectual pursuits after the performance of home and social duties are difficult questions to settle, and constitute serious problems to many an earnest, thoughtful girl; yet they must be decided, for self-education is a duty of the gravest import (Goslett, 1892).

But while girls should be serious about improving their minds, they should always be aware of the need to preserve their femininity, and many Victorian commentators thought that too much learning of the wrong sort would damage it. By an exclusive attention to the solid branches, and in a high degree, the character is rendered too masculine. There is need of the softening influence of those pursuits which are designed chiefly to embellish (Nicholson, 1850).

Many Victorian commentators on girls' education insisted that the only reason girls should learn anything at all about "masculine" subjects was so they could become better listeners when in male company. For example, Mrs. Ellis in *The Daughters of England* told readers that science, if studied for its own sake, would damage their "feminine delicacy." Scientific studies were only justifiable as part of their education because such knowledge would render them more companionable to men. Mrs. Ellis emphasized that possessing such knowledge did not mean that a girl should display it. "I must again observe, it is by no means necessary that we should talk much on any of these subjects" (Ellis, 1843).

Article source: Gorham, D. (1982). *The Victorian girl and the feminine ideal.* London: Croom Helm Publishing. Reprinted with permission.

HISTORICAL BACKGROUND

TIMELINE OF WOMEN'S RIGHTS 1860–1920

1869	Wyoming Territory becomes first modern political entity to grant vote to women. It becomes first U.S. state to do so when it is admitted to Union (1890).
1869	Female lawyers are licensed in United States.
1878	U.S. constitutional amendment to grant full suffrage to women is introduced in Congress. (It is introduced every year until its passage in 1920.)
1912	National American Women's Suffrage Association organizes congressional committee to campaign for federal amendment to give equal rights to women.
1919	Nineteenth Amendment to United Constitution, extending vote to women, passes. (It is ratified in 1920.)
1920	League of Women Voters is founded to educate women in use of their suffrage. Men are admitted after 1974.
1920	All U.S. states allow women to practice law by this date.

Reprinted with permission of Macmillan General Reference USA, a division of Ahsuce, Inc. from THE NEW YORK PUBLIC LIBRARY BOOK OF CHRONOLOGY by Bruce Wetterau. Copyright © 1990 Bruce Wetterau.

UNIT PLANNING PROCEDURES AND GUIDESHEETS

The unit planning guidesheet is a blueprint of the unit plan that describes the separate components and provides an overview of the completed product. Because the project is a research-based inductive activity, it is not developed in a linear fashion. Each of the sections are drafted by the student group, receive feedback from the instructor, and are revised as needed throughout the curriculum development process. Guidesheets for each of the sections of the plan clearly describe the task, and rubrics identify the criteria used for assessment.

UNIT PLAN GRADING CRITERIA

Team Members: **Date:** _____

_____   **Section:** _____

_____   **Score:** _____

_____

_____

_____

Integration

A variety of content matter is planned.   (2) _____
The content is consistent with the literature.   (2) _____
The integration statement identifies skills, content, and processes. (2) _____

Activities

The activities cause students to think critically.   (1) _____
The activities encourage problem solving.   (1) _____
The activities are appropriate for students on a variety of levels. (2) _____

Format

The objectives are consistent with the evaluation statements.   (2) _____
The fact sheets are consistent with the activities.   (2) _____
The tracking instruments are consistent with the objectives
    and the evaluation statements.   (2) _____
The handouts are appropriate.   (2) _____
The bibliography is appropriate.   (1) _____

Delegation of Responsibilities

The work is fairly distributed.   (1) _____

Total   (20) _____

Comments

UNIT PLANNING GUIDESHEET

This is a description of the sections that are required for the unit plan. Creativity is valued so this list should be seen as the *minimum* requirements that form the foundation for the unit assignment. We suggest that your team approach the construction of your unit plan in a personal way, so that the talents and skills of each member of the team are reflected in the final product.

Literature Concept

The literature concept is a statement about the woman of achievement followed by a problem that is the central focus of the curriculum in the unit plan. The literature concept links the core text to the instructional content. The problem prepares the instructor and students for inductive, interactive, cooperative learning.

Integration Statement

The integration statement identifies the skills, content, and processes taught in the unit plan. It is the last section of the plan to be completed and is revised after the unit is taught.

Objectives

The objectives are stated as performance-based teaching objectives. The teacher first identifies the teaching objective and lists outcomes on increasingly difficult cognitive levels. Performance-based objectives are written content free so they can be used again with other units of study.

Materials

This section of the plan identifies materials used in the instruction. Similar to the integration statement, it is one of the last parts of the plan to be completed.

Motivation

In this stage of the instruction, the teacher prepares the students for learning. The motivation can contain questions that enable the teacher to check for background knowledge, an activity that causes children to hypothesize about an issue to be resolved, or a class experience that provides schema for the unit curriculum.

Procedure

The procedure is the first stage of the planning process and the link between the core text and the interdisciplinary activities. In your group, decide how the text will be used. Will it be read orally by the teacher, read by the students, or used as a resource? Then, reflect on the beginning, middle, and end of the instruction. This organizational design should suggest a sequence for the unit activities. How will you prepare students for learning? What content should be introduced first? What will you use for a closure activity? Each activity should be described briefly, labeled, and sequenced in logical order.

(continued)

(continued)

Fact Sheet(s)

The fact sheets identify the subject area concepts to be taught in the unit plan. Concepts can be drawn from encyclopedias or science, social studies, math, or language textbooks. List the concepts and label them by subject area. Similar to the integration statement, this section of the unit plan is revised after the unit is taught.

Handouts

These are attachments of webs, graphic organizers, and guidesheets used by students during the instruction.

Evaluation

The evaluation statements must correspond directly to each of the objectives and should be activity based.

Assessment Tracking Instruments

How will you track students' mastery of content, process, or skill performance? This section can contain student conference sheets, status sheets used by the teacher, or student self-reporting forms.

Bibliography

The bibliography is written in APA format and contains a listing of the books and materials used with the unit plan. Teachers' resources and student materials are grouped separately.

Delegation of Responsibilities

In this section, identify how the members of your group delegated the responsibility for the unit plan. Which roles were assumed by which individuals? What was the rationale for this decision?

GROUPING GUIDESHEET

For each of the projects you submit in class, you will be asked to report how your group organized the project and what roles were assumed by individual group members. To assist with these decisions, hold a meeting with your group.

1. Identify the strengths of each group member.

2. Appoint a group leader and exchange addresses, telephone numbers, and e-mail addresses. Based on the talents of the individual group members, the group leader assigns roles, establishes a timetable, sets meeting dates, and identifies meeting sites.

3. Cooperative Group Roles

Researcher	After an initial meeting with the group, the researcher locates and copies source material, compiles the bibliographic information, and reviews concepts orally with colleagues.
Drafters	The two drafters listen to the ideas of other group members, read the source material, and use the project guidelines to synthesize content into a product that is distributed to the researcher, editor, and computer specialist.
Computer Specialist	The computer specialist works with the editor to identify the format of the product, check the grammar, design the graphics, copy and distribute segments of the product to group members, and monitor the circulation of resource materials.
Editor	The editor works closely with the computer specialist in making decisions in the refinement of the final product. In the initial meeting with group members, the editor records opinions of group members and uses these suggestions as the guide for the editing process.

The role of group leader should rotate among group members for the different class projects. In today's elementary schools, teachers are being asked to take a more active part in making curricular decisions. One of the objectives of the group projects is to help you to become comfortable with the collaboration process. To collaborate successfully, group members must listen actively to the suggestions of others, contribute to the completion of a common project, synthesize data to meet preestablished guidelines, and assume leadership in the designing of instruction. An effective group also establishes respect and trust in fellow group members.

AMERICAN WOMEN OF ACHIEVEMENT

RESEARCH TOPICS SIGN-UP SHEET

Write the names of your group on the lines with the famous American you have chosen to research. List your section under the female's occupation.

Marian Anderson
singer

_____

_____

_____

_____

Margaret Bourke-White
photographer

_____

_____

_____

_____

Katharine Hepburn
actress

_____

_____

_____

_____

Mahalia Jackson
gospel singer

_____

_____

_____

_____

Helen Keller
humanitarian

_____

_____

_____

_____

(continued)

Georgia O'Keeffe
artist

_____

_____

_____

_____

Wilma Rudolph
athlete

_____

_____

_____

_____

Mary Cassatt
artist

_____

_____

_____

_____

Julia Morgan
architect

_____

_____

_____

_____

Grandma Moses
artist

_____

_____

_____

_____

(continued)

(continued)

Louise Nevelson
sculptor

_____

_____

_____

_____

Ethel Barrymore
actress

_____

_____

_____

_____

Agnes de Mille
choreographer

_____

_____

_____

_____

Isadora Duncan
dancer

_____

_____

_____

_____

Helen Hayes
actress

_____

_____

_____

_____

(continued)

Elizabeth Blackwell
physician

_____

_____

_____

_____

Rachel Carson
biologist

_____

_____

_____

_____

Barbara McClintock
biologist

_____

_____

_____

_____

Margaret Mead
anthropologist

_____

_____

_____

_____

Eleanor Roosevelt
diplomat

_____

_____

_____

_____

(continued)

(continued)

Emma Goldman
political activist

_____

_____

_____

_____

Emily Dickenson
poet

_____

_____

_____

_____

Edna St. Vincent Millay
poet

_____

_____

_____

_____

Gertrude Stein
author

_____

_____

_____

_____

Florence Sabin
medical researcher

_____

_____

_____

_____

UNIT RESOURCES

Life in the Period

Barmeier, J. (1997). *Manners and customs.* Philadelphia: Chelsea House Publishers.

Ciment, J. (1995). *Law and order.* Philadelphia: Chelsea House Publishers.

Leuzzi, L. (1995a). *Transportation.* Philadelphia: Chelsea House Publishers.

Leuzzi, L. (1995b). *Urban life.* Philadelphia: Chelsea House Publishers.

Ritchie, D. (1996). *Frontier life.* Philadelphia: Chelsea House Publishers.

Ritchie, D., & Israel, F. (1995). *Health and medicine.* Philadelphia: Chelsea House Publishers.

The Proper Victorian Lady

Bender, B. (1993). Darwin, and the "natural history of doctresses": The sex war between Howells, Phelips, Jewett, and James. *Prospects, 18,* 81–120.

Brown, V. B. (1990). The fear of feminization: Los Angeles high schools in the progressive era. *Feminist Studies, 16*(3), 493–518.

Cargan, L., & Melko, M. (1982). *Singles: Myths and realities.* Beverly Hills, CA: Sage Publications.

Chambers-Schiller, L. (1978). The single woman reformer: Conflicts between family and vocation, 1830–1860. *Frontiers, 3*(3), 41–47.

Gorham, D. (1982). *The Victorian girl and the feminine ideal.* Bloomington, IN: Indiana University Press.

Green, H. (1983). *The light of the home.* New York: Pantheon Books.

Kornfeld, K., & Kornfeld, S. (1987). The female bildungsroman in nineteenth-century America: Parameters of a vision. *Journal of American Culture, 10*(4), 69–75.

McDannell, C. (1986). *The Christian home in Victorian America, 1840–1900.* Bloomington, IN: Indiana University Press.

Pildes, J. (1978). Mothers and daughters: Understanding the roles. *Frontiers, 3*(2), 1–11.

Rosenzweig, L. W. (1991). "The anchor of my life": Middle class American mothers and college-educated daughters 1880–1920. *Journal of Social History, 25*(1), 5–25.

Seller, M. S. (1975). Beyond the stereotype: A new look at the immigrant woman. *Journal of Ethnic Studies, 3*(1), 59–70.

Stearns, P. (1993). Girls, boys, and emotions: Redefinitions and historical change. *Journal of American History, 80*(1), 36–74.

Stern, D., Smith, S., & Doolittle, F. (1975). How children used to work. *Law and Contemporary Problems, 39*(3), 93–117.

Vandenberg-Daves, J. (1992). The manly pursuit of a partnership between the sexes: The debate over YMCA programs for women and girls, 1914–1933. *Journal of American History, 74*(4), 1324–1346.

Wright, G. (1980). *Moralism and the model home.* Chicago: The University of Chicago Press.

American Women of Achievement Biographies

Berry, M. (1988). *Georgia O'Keeffe.* Philadelphia: Chelsea House Publishers.

Biracree, T. (1988). *Wilma Rudolph.* Philadelphia: Chelsea House Publishers.

Biracree, T. (1989). *Grandma Moses.* Philadelphia: Chelsea House Publishers.

(continued)

(continued)

Brown, J. (1989). *Elizabeth Blackwell.* Philadelphia: Chelsea House Publishers.
Cain, M. (1989a). *Louise Nevelson.* Philadelphia: Chelsea House Publishers.
Cain, M. (1989b). *Mary Cassatt.* Philadelphia: Chelsea House Publishers.
Cary, J. (1990). *Julia Morgan.* Philadelphia: Chelsea House Publishers.
Daffron, C. (1988). *Margaret Bourke-White.* Philadelphia: Chelsea House Publishers.
Daffron, C. (1989). *Edna St. Vincent Millay.* Philadelphia: Chelsea House Publishers.
Jezer, M. (1988). *Rachel Carson.* Philadelphia: Chelsea House Publishers.
Kettredge, M. (1990). *Helen Hayes.* Phildelphia: Chelsea House Publishers.
Kettredge, M. (1991). *Barbara McClintock.* Philadelphia: Chelsea House Publishers.
Kozoday, R. (1988). *Isadora Duncan.* Phildelphia: Chelsea House Publishers.
La Farge, A. (1988). *Gertrude Stein.* Phildelphia: Chelsea House Publishers.
Lantham, C. (1988). *Katharine Hepburn.* Phildelphia: Chelsea House Publishers.
Olsen, V. (1990). *Emily Dickenson.* Phildelphia: Chelsea House Publishers.
Shore, N. (1987). *Amelia Earhart.* Phildelphia: Chelsea House Publishers.
Speaker-Yuan, M. (1990). *Agnes de Mille.* Philadelphia: Chelsea House Publishers.
Tedards, A. (1988). *Marion Anderson.* Philadelphia: Chelsea House Publishers.
Thorleifson, A. (1991). *Ethyl Barrymore.* Philadelphia: Chelsea House Publishers.
Toor, R. (1989). *Eleanor Roosevelt.* Philadelphia: Chelsea House Publishers.
Waldstreicher, D. (1990). *Emma Goldman.* Philadelphia: Chelsea House Publishers.
Wepman, D. (1987). *Helen Keller.* Philadelphia: Chelsea House Publishers.
Wolfe, C. (1990). *Mahalia Jackson.* Philadelphia: Chelsea House Publishers.
Ziesk, E. (1990). *Margaret Mead.* Philadelphia: Chelsea House Publishers.

CLOSURE STATEMENT

At this step in the planning process, the teacher has ensured that the unit topic is consistent with the teaching objectives identified for the school year. Resources have been checked to make sure that library materials are readily available for student research. After reviewing the materials, the teacher decides which sources can be used as the initial reading assignment and the core text for the unit. The core text should be interesting, short in length, and contain authentic material and illustrations. Many biographies can be used to gather information, but the most useful in stimulating critical thinking are those that play the subject against the social context.

REFERENCES

Ellis, S. S. (1843). *The daughters of England, their position in society, character, and responsibilities.* London: Fischer, Son & Co.

Gorham, D. (1982). *The Victorian girl and the feminine ideal.* London: Croom Helm Publishing.

Goslett, C. (1892). *The duty of girls in regard to self-education, our mothers and daughters* (as cited in Gorham, D., 1982).

Nicholson, W. (1850). *How to be a lady* (as cited in Gorham, D., 1982).

Tilt, E. J. (1852). *Elements of health, and principles of female hygiene.* London: Henry G. Bohn.

CHAPTER

ORGANIZATIONAL ACTIVITIES: THE LITERATURE SYNOPSIS AND PLANNING WHEEL

Chapter 4 explains the importance of the literature synopsis and the planning wheel in the development of elementary or middle school curriculum. The prototype unit, Amelia Earhart, is used to model a completed wheel.

Planning curricula is an exciting undertaking because teachers must consider the skill levels and interests of the children in the class before designing assignments. In matching the content to the class, subject matter should be examined as a whole before deciding how it will be sequenced into assignment segments.

■ How do teachers convert research into elementary school curriculum?

Organizational Activities

Constructing Materials
- Guidesheets
- Rubrics

Unit Plan Prototype
- Women of Achievement Unit Plan—Amelia Earhart
- Literature Synopsis Grading Criteria
- Literature Synopsis Guidesheet
- Historical Background

The Planning Wheel
- Identifying the Problem
- Evaluating the Problem
- Selecting Subject Matter Headings for Integration
- Listing Content Concepts Under Subject Headings
- Developing Focus Questions
- Example—Amelia Earhart Planning Wheel
- Grading Criteria

CONSTRUCTING MATERIALS

Guidesheets

Begin by developing a series of questions that are the essence of the content. Questions are useful in providing focus to the instruction and guiding research. We have found that guidesheets at each phase of the project clarify the instructor's intentions and provide a mental picture of the expected product.

Elementary and middle school students, though eager to please, tend to view success in terms of black and white. Many are afraid to take risks because they do not want to make a mistake or submit a product that has an error. By developing guidesheets, the teacher leads but does not control the final product. Students are more creative because they have a tangible image of the instructor's expectations.

Rubrics

It is also important that elementary students monitor the quality of the work they submit. A rubric explains how the teacher will assess the product. If the rubric is given to students with the guidesheet, it becomes a valuable tool in the final editing process. The ultimate objective of all teachers is to lead students into independence. When given a target, students feel more confident, enjoy projects more, and are much more likely to create successful products.

UNIT PLAN PROTOTYPE

Women of Achievement Unit Plan—Amelia Earhart

After the Women of Achievement core text is read, the curriculum developers identify characteristics that made the subject (Amelia Earhart in the prototype) unique in her lifetime. This is done by comparing information reported about typical family life in the time period to the life of the female that was chosen as the research focus. Information is synthesized into a short paper that becomes the core of the unit. The following sample guidesheets are examples of supportive materials that could be adapted to guide the project and clarify the objectives.

LITERATURE SYNOPSIS GRADING CRITERIA

Team Members:

Date: _____

_____

Section: _____

_____

Score: _____

_____

_____

_____

Introduction

Accurate background information is documented. (5) _____

Literature Synopsis

Key events are identified. (2) _____
Key events are interpreted. (2) _____
Logical conclusions are drawn. (2) _____
Influences are described. (2) _____
Contributions are described. (2) _____

Composition

The composition shows good mechanics, grammar, and spelling. (1) _____
The composition reflects clear, concise expression. (1) _____

Bibliography

The bibliography is in the correct format. (2) _____

Delegation of Responsibility

The work is fairly distributed. (1) _____

Total

(20) _____

Comments

LITERATURE SYNOPSIS GUIDESHEET

The literature synopsis consists of four to six typed pages of text containing the following sections.

Introduction

The introduction provides the background information that the reader of the paper needs to know to understand the content. It is written from an objective viewpoint and supported with library resources. In this section of the paper, discuss some of the following issues:

■ What type of aspirations did parents have for their children in the period from 1860 to 1920?
■ What were the typical family and societal roles for females during this period?
■ What occupations were available to unmarried females?

Synopsis

The synopsis contains an analytical summary of the biographical content. It is written from the reader's point of view. It answers the following questions:

■ How was the biographical subject different from the typical woman of the period?
■ What person or event in the subject's childhood influenced this difference?
■ How did the subject influence the period? How did the period influence the subject?
■ What strategies did the subject use to overcome impediments to her ideas, craft, talent, or innovations?

Bibliography

The bibliography lists information about the source materials used in writing the paper. It is written in APA format.

Delegation of Responsibilities

In this section, describe how your group worked together in completing the assignment.

HISTORICAL BACKGROUND

AMELIA EARHART

Amelia Earhart was born in Atchison, Kansas, in 1897. On May 20, 1932, an Irish farmer standing in his field watched in astonishment as a plane landed among his cows. A woman jumped from the plane, smiled, and said cheerfully, "I've come from America."

Amelia Earhart hadn't made it to her intended destination, Paris, because of mechanical problems; she was, nevertheless, the first woman to fly solo across the Atlantic, and she had beaten the record time.

As much notice as the transatlantic trip brought her, Earhart is probably most famous for the trip she didn't make: the 1937 flight around the world. Her disappearance near Howland Island in the Pacific Ocean has been the subject of myths since the day it happened. Some speculate that she landed safely on another island and remained stranded there. Others think she was shot down by the Japanese because she was secretly spying for the United States Navy. Still others believe she was kidnapped by aliens.

The speculation over Earhart's death sometimes obscures her accomplishments. She was a pioneer in a dangerous field who prized her skill and independence, and had married only on her own terms. She had contempt for women who used their gender to get special treatment. From the time in her childhood when she received a football and a rifle from her father to the time in her adulthood when her plane went down near Howland Island, she fought against the system of "dividing people according to their gender, and putting them in little feminine or masculine pigeonholes."

Used with permission of Sterling Publishing Co., Inc., 387 Park Ave. S. NY, NY 10016 from REMEMBER THE LADIES by Kirstin Olsen, © 1988 by Kirstin Olsen.

THE PLANNING WHEEL

The planning wheel is a blueprint that allows teachers to analyze the content and select concepts that will become the major segments of the instruction. The first step in this process is to identify a major problem or the core of the unit.

Identifying the Problem

Begin by making a statement about the research subject.

EXAMPLE   Amelia Earhart was a risk taker who defied the conventions of her era to become a role model for women who wanted careers in male-oriented occupations.

Follow the statement with a problem that requires the gathering and analysis of information. The problem needs to be broad and open ended because it is to be the center of the web and the core concept of the unit.

EXAMPLE   Why did Amelia Earhart become a hero to the American public when so many other nontraditional women were criticized and rejected?

The statement and the problem are written in the center of the graphic organizer and are included in the unit plan as the literature concept.

LITERATURE CONCEPT

Amelia Earhart was a risk taker who defied the conventions of her era to become a role model for women who wanted careers in male-oriented occupations. Why did Amelia become a hero to the American public when so many other nontraditional women were criticized and rejected?

Evaluating the Problem

Evaluate the depth of your concept by answering the following questions:

1. Is the problem open ended?
2. Does it require students to compare information from several different sources?
3. To solve the problem, do students have to form an opinion and back up their conclusions with documentation?
4. Do students need to compare, reflect, and hypothesize about the facts before stating their opinions in response to the problem?

Selecting Subject Matter Headings for Integration

Decisions about subject matter integration should flow naturally from the biography. The curriculum developers should brainstorm a list of the events in the life of the subject. These events may be listed on a timeline and appear in the appendix of the unit plan. Examine the timeline and try to think about what background information would be meaningful to students in understanding the subject and the period of time in which she lived.

Do not feel confined by traditional subject matter (reading, writing, math, social studies, language arts) taught during the school day. Teachers are more familiar with these topics, and have a tendency to want to force all information into these subject matter headings. Integrated units are based on concepts that are learned more easily and thoroughly when teachers do a needs assessment to determine students' background, build a knowledge base through an experience or modeling, and check for understanding by having the concepts applied to a new situation. Biology, sociology, geography, art, music, or physical education can be used effectively as subject headings if they provide background for the plot. These decisions are driven by the biography in the core text. The rationale for introducing these concepts is to enhance understanding of the biography while providing a context for subject matter content that will be explained in depth at a later time.

Listing Content Concepts Under Subject Headings

Once the headings have been identified, content concepts must be selected, instruction must be sequenced, and the activities must be planned. Since decisions have not been made about the amount and depth of information to be included, only the major concepts are listed on the graphic organizer under subject matter headings. The web may be thought of as a draft because it may be edited after gathering information for the fact sheet.

Developing Focus Questions

The focus questions prioritize the information and enable curriculum developers to agree on the issues that are most important for students to grasp. The number of questions are determined by the ages and abilities of the students. Younger students will have fewer questions. The first question will probably be written at the knowledge level because a base of information will have to be mastered before students are able to engage in problem solving. Two or three other questions should challenge students to compare, contrast, synthesize, and hypothesize information in their journey to the solution of the core problem.

EXAMPLE   Who was Amelia Earhart and what were her lifetime achievements?

How would Amelia's life have been different if she lived in our lifetime rather than in the past?

What elements of Amelia's personality caused her to be different?
How do these characteristics compare to leadership qualities?
How did they contribute to her disappearance?

EXAMPLE—AMELIA EARHART PLANNING WHEEL

Focus Questions

Who was Amelia Earhart and what were her lifetime achievements?

How would Amelia's life have been different if she had lived in our lifetime rather than in the past?

What elements of Amelia's personality caused her to be different? How do these characteristics compare to leadership qualities? How did they contribute to her disappearance?

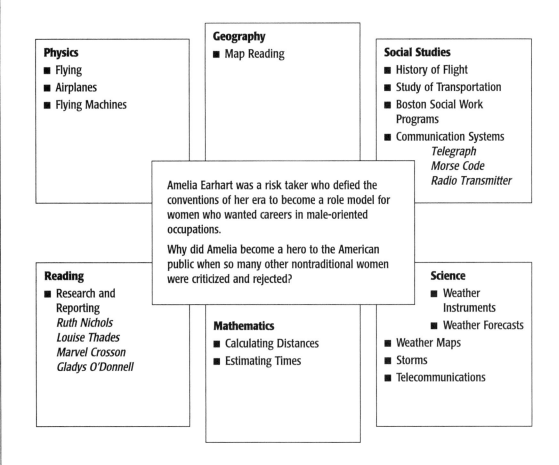

Physics
- Flying
- Airplanes
- Flying Machines

Geography
- Map Reading

Social Studies
- History of Flight
- Study of Transportation
- Boston Social Work Programs
- Communication Systems
  Telegraph
  Morse Code
  Radio Transmitter

Amelia Earhart was a risk taker who defied the conventions of her era to become a role model for women who wanted careers in male-oriented occupations.

Why did Amelia become a hero to the American public when so many other nontraditional women were criticized and rejected?

Reading
- Research and Reporting
  Ruth Nichols
  Louise Thades
  Marvel Crosson
  Gladys O'Donnell

Mathematics
- Calculating Distances
- Estimating Times

Science
- Weather Instruments
- Weather Forecasts
- Weather Maps
- Storms
- Telecommunications

INTERDISCIPLINARY PLANNING WHEEL

GRADING CRITERIA

Team Members: **Date:** _____

_____   **Section:** _____

_____

_____

_____

Content Subject Headings

    Broad content is covered.   (4) _____

Content Concepts

    Subject matter is diverse.   (4) _____
    Biography is consistent.   (4) _____

Essential Questions

    Focus for content concepts is provided.   (4) _____
    Critical thinking is stimulated.   (4) _____

Total   (20) _____

Comments

CLOSURE STATEMENT

The synopsis and the planning wheel are organizational tools for the teacher or the group of teachers planning the instruction. If the curriculum is being implemented in a departmentalized setting, the teachers responsible for the content components can use the literature synopsis and the planning wheel as guides when selecting materials and determining content emphasis.

The planning wheel may be edited or modified when completing other sections of the unit or after teaching the unit for the first time. However, the purpose of the wheel is to synthesize and organize the content, to provide clarity and focus to the instruction, and to serve as a reference when making other curricular decisions.

CHAPTER 5

RESEARCH AND FACT FINDING: THE FACT SHEET

Chapter 5 identifies the purpose and the procedures used in constructing a fact sheet. A sample grading criteria and example are provided for clarification. The example is based on information relating to the Amelia Earhart unit.

To understand a topic, concept, or a theme in depth, it must be analyzed both globally and specifically. The planning wheel provides an overview of the unit and identifies the major concepts that will be taught. Fact finding is the next task to be completed. In this step of the planning process, the teacher gathers the content knowledge taught through the activities in the procedure section. The fact sheet supplements the information written in the literature synopsis by providing details that will enrich the instruction and lead to a more in-depth understanding of the issues affecting the problem.

■ What information is needed to provide the resources for the development of the concepts listed on the planning wheel?

■ What supplementary materials are available in the school and the community?

Research and Fact Finding:
Relationship of the Content to the Problem

The Fact Sheet
■ Informational Sources
■ Purpose of the Fact Sheet

Fact Sheet Materials
■ Fact Sheet Grading Criteria
■ Fact Sheet Example

THE FACT SHEET

Information Sources

The planning wheel identifies the subject matter and the concepts that will be integrated into the study of the core problem. The next task is to gather background information in the related content areas. The school librarian can be of great help with this task. Encyclopedias, newspapers, journals, books, and basal series can be used in the information gathering process.

Purpose of the Fact Sheet

Once the unit is implemented, students will be contributing to the facts gathered and the teacher needs to be prepared to include students' contributions in the discussion. For this reason, background information related to the core problem is gathered well in advance and listed on the fact sheet.

While selecting appropriate topics for integration, you should consider the attention spans, skill levels, and ages of the students and decide how much information should be shared in each of the related subject areas. We would not expect elementary students to understand physics as thoroughly as a high school junior, but a discussion and demonstration of the lift produced by an airplane wing could stimulate interest in knowing how airplanes operate. Information introduced in the context of an interesting unit could lead to a deeper understanding of physics later in the students' academic development.

Relationship of the Concepts to the Problem

Understanding flight and weather is also important to the solution of the core problem. If students know how the lift is affected by air pressure and weather, we can assume that a flight with only minimal ability to contact ground stations or ships at sea would be very dangerous in uncertain weather. Students can hypothesize about the motivation for Amelia Earhart's decision to continue the flight without the radio antenna or telegraph key and imagine what events triggered her disappearance. Was this decision consistent or inconsistent with what we know about her behavior throughout her life? Even though Amelia's final flight ended in tragedy, she left a legacy for all women by opening new opportunities and shattering the concept of women as helpless creatures.

Some of the subject matter is included because it is consistent with the curriculum guidelines of the school district. Other information is introduced because it leads to deeper understanding of the core problem, stimulates interest in the topic, or builds a foundation for concepts that will be developed later in the students' academic program.

The purpose of the fact sheet is to establish parameters for the concepts that will be developed in each of the subject matter areas. However, you will want to have this information readily available once the teaching begins. After locating background facts, list them under headings on the fact sheet. The fact sheet should be thought of as a draft because it is often necessary to add additional information as the activities in the procedure section are being designed.

FACT SHEET GRADING CRITERIA

Team Members: **Date:** _____

_____   **Section:** _____

_____

_____

_____

Subject Matter Concepts

Concepts are thoroughly researched.   (5) _____
Concepts are clearly stated.   (5) _____
Concepts are consistent with core problem.   (5) _____

Delegation of Responsibility   (5) _____

Comments

AMELIA EARHART FACT SHEET

Social Studies

HISTORY OF FLIGHT

1200s	The Chinese used kites to spy on their enemies.
1738	Daniel Bernoulli discovered the airfoil. The principle behind the airfoil was that the increasing movement of a gas or liquid lowers its pressure.
1783	Montgolfier invented the first hot-air balloon designed to carry passengers. The French balloon carried its passengers five miles on the initial flight.
1783	Shortly after Montgolfier's flight, Jacques Charles successfully piloted the first hydrogen balloon.
1849	Sir George Cayley flew a child in the first glider. Four years later, Cayley's coachman became the first adult glider passenger and, upon landing, resigned his job.
1852	French engineer Henri Giffard invented the first steam-powered airship.
1903	The Wright brothers flew the first powered airplane at Kitty Hawk, North Carolina.
1907	The first gasoline powered helicopter took flight in France. The helicopter was invented by Paul Cornu. It took about 30 years to perfect a reliable helicopter.
1908	Glenn Hammond Curtiss, an American inventor and aviation pioneer, made the first public flights in the United States. He also established the first flying school in 1909 and made a breathtaking flight from Albany to New York City.
1909	Louis Bl'eriot, a French aviator and inventor, was the first aviator to cross the English Channel in a heavier-than-air machine.
1911	Glenn Hammond Curtiss invented ailerons and, after World War I, made radical advances in the design of planes and their motors.
1922	Anton Herman Gerard was a German-American aircraft manufacturer who owned factories in Germany that produced the triplanes and bi-planes used in World War I. An inventor who developed the mechanism that allowed machine-gun bullets to be fired through a rotating propeller without hitting the blades, Gerard also developed the first commercial aircraft.

Science

WEATHER INSTRUMENTS

Meteorology	Meteorology is the science that studies atmospheric patterns and weather.

(continued)

Forecast	Forecast is a future prediction of the weather based on observation and analysis of atmospheric conditions. The forecast describes what is most likely to happen. Meteorologists (scientists who study weather) make these predictions by measuring wind temperature, air pressure, wind speed, and wind direction.
Weather vane	A weather vane is a movable device attached to a pole that shows wind direction.
Anemometer	An anemometer measures wind speed. Cups catch the wind making the anemometer's arms spin. As the arms spin, the wind speed can be measured.
Wind sock	A wind sock shows both wind speed and wind direction. It looks like a cloth cone open at both ends. The wind sock twists on a pole showing the direction of the wind. If the sock is blowing straight out, it shows the wind is blowing strongly. If the sock is limp, there is little wind.
Relative humidity	Relative humidity is the amount of water vapor in the air compared to the greatest amount of water vapor the air can hold at that temperature. Warm air can hold more water vapor than cold air. Relative humidity is stated as a percent and is measured with a wet and dry bulb thermometer.

WEATHER FORECASTS

Air mass	An air mass is a large body of air extending hundreds or thousands of miles horizontally and sometimes as high as the stratosphere. An air mass has the same amount of moisture and humidity throughout. The weather in a certain area of land is determined by the air mass. Changes in the weather occur when air masses move.
Front	A front is the boundary between two air masses that are not alike. When cold air moves into a warmer air mass, it is called a cold front.
Jet streams	Jet streams are high speed ribbons of air that influence the movement of air masses. Jet streams move from west to east or from north to south in a wavelike motion.

WEATHER MAP

Isotherm	An isotherm is a line drawn on a weather map connecting areas that have the same temperature.
Isobar	An isobar is a line drawn on a weather map connecting areas that have the same air pressure. Air pressure is given in units called millibars. An area of high pressure brings fair weather; low pressure brings cloudy weather.

(continued)

(continued)

STORMS

Thunderstorm   Thunderstorms are caused by rapidly rising updrafts of warm air that contain large amounts of water vapor. Condensation occurs as the warm air rises and cools causing the water vapor to crystalize and form a cloud. A cool air current (downdraft) causes the moisture to fall to the earth in the form of rain or hail.

Tornado   A tornado is a violent, destructive whirling wind accompanied by a funnel-shaped cloud that travels in a narrow path over the land. No one knows exactly what causes tornadoes. In a tornado, a layer of warm humid air close to the ground becomes trapped by a layer of cold, dry air above it. Then, a rapidly moving cold front moves into the region. The cold front lifts the warm air between the two layers of cold air. The warm air breaks through the cold air and rushes upward in the form of a twisting mass called the tornado funnel.

Hurricane   A hurricane is a violent storm that develops over the ocean in a tropical area. Hurricanes are usually accompanied by rains, thunder, lightning, and winds up to 74 miles per hour. Hurricanes contain a rotating mass of air with a low pressure center. Each hurricane has a calm region in the center called the eye of the storm. The strongest winds of the hurricane rotate around the eye.

PHYSICS

Flight   Balloons and airships are heavier than air and fly by generating a force that overcomes their weight and supports them in the air. Kites use the power of wind to keep them aloft. All winged aircraft, including gliders and helicopters, make use of the airfoil and its lifting power. Vertical takeoff aircraft direct the power of their jet engines downward and heave themselves off the ground by brute force.

　　The two principles that govern heavier-than-air flight are the same as those that propel powered vessels—action and reaction, and suction. When applied to flight, suction is known as lift.

Airfoil   The cross-section of a wing has a shape called airfoil. As the wing moves through the air, the air divides to pass around the wing. The airfoil is curved so that air passing above the wing moves faster than the air passing beneath. Fast-moving air has a lower pressure than slow-moving air. The pressure of the air is therefore greater beneath the wing than above it. This difference in air pressure forces the wing upward. The force is called lift.

CLOSURE STATEMENT

The fact sheet provides the depth to the unit of study. If the core problem or theme of the unit was selected using curriculum guides or standards in the planning stage, some of the information taught may already be included in the science, social studies, or reading texts. The fact sheet need only include information that is not readily available in the texts and must be researched from other sources. After the unit has been taught and you have observed students' responses to the instruction, the fact sheet should be reviewed to determine if the concepts need to be modified.

CHAPTER

6

DESIGNING INSTRUCTION

Chapter 6 shows the logical connection between the unit motivation, the strategies listed in the procedure section, and the guidesheets attached to the appendix. Sample motivational activities, curriculum strategies, and guidesheets are provided.

Learning is a risk-taking adventure. If students are to be successful, they must be made to feel that there is no penalty for exploring and hypothesizing before a conclusion is drawn. Planning instruction that stimulates the most advanced student without frustrating the weakest is a talent. Teachers accomplish this objective by preparing students to learn, giving clear directions through guidesheets, planning challenging projects, and observing learning behaviors so that gaps in understanding can be addressed. Designing instruction is a very exciting activity.

■ How do successful teachers plan curriculum that moves smoothly from readiness to new concept development to application?

Designing Instruction

Motivation
- The Importance of Readiness
- The Motivational Activity
- Action Research
- Guidesheets

The Procedures and Appendix
- Creating Activities and Guidesheets
- Sample Activities
- Sample Appendix

THE IMPORTANCE OF READINESS

If we are designing a unit and one of the goals is to foster collaboration, it is important to prepare students for the instruction. Because students can have very different background experiences, clear directions and support before assigning a task can make the difference between success and failure. It is unrealistic for a teacher to introduce an activity without checking to see if students have the background knowledge necessary to complete the task. Most collaborative activities involve problem solving through application of a knowledge base. Time spent in readiness results in more confident, enthusiastic students and greater success in problem solving. In sequencing the activities in your unit of study, it is wise to introduce concepts and check for understanding before assigning a task that involves application of the information. The needs assessment activity can involve the construction of a graphic organizer (for example, a Venn diagram comparing the lives of women in 1900 to the lives of women today); a discussion (for example, discuss with a partner everything you know about the dangers of flight); or an activity (for example, bring in photographs of women living in the early 1900s and draw one conclusion about life in the period based on the photographs). Students' responses indicate the depth of their background experience and provide insight into the level of preparation that is needed.

To further clarify the multitextual unit design, we have created sample motivation and procedure sections that demonstrate activities for a class of elementary or middle school students researching American Women of Achievement.

The Motivational Activity

After gathering the information for the fact sheet, the teacher plans a motivational activity that will stimulate interest in the topic and provide a knowledge base for the unit. In the example unit, it is important that students have some understanding of how life was different for women in the past if they are to recognize the leadership qualities of the American Women of Achievement. An action research project is an example of a motivational activity that can be used to ensure that students have some background information about family roles in the early part of the century. A motivational activity, however, is not limited to action research. It could involve viewing a video, inspecting and hypothesizing about a table of realia from the period, or visiting a museum. The idea is to involve students and spark their interest in a topic. However, creative teachers recognize that the more real and meaningful the teacher makes the motivational experience, the greater the enthusiasm for in-depth study.

Action Research

In an action research project, students gather information from real sources in the community to contribute to the solution of a problem. The information gathered can be used to stimulate discussion, to compare with data published on the topic in journals or newspapers, or as background information to be used in the development of a survey.

Preparation for this activity begins with a discussion of how we can be sure the information we gather is accurate. We can ask an expert, we can compare the information with opinions printed in reputable journals, or we can check for consensus. An expert is someone who is charged with making decisions in the area of the topic. Checking the group that supports its publication can identify a reputable journal. In determining consensus, a survey will show us how many individuals agree or disagree with an opinion.

If this activity is followed to conclusion, it can result in the writing of a position paper in which students form an opinion and support the opinion with facts. In this instance, we would not complete the entire process but modify the assignment by having small groups of students create a series of questions about life in the past that would be asked of residents in a retirement home.

MOTIVATION STATEMENT

After completing a KWL chart, students will develop a series of questions to ask retirement home residents about family roles, educational opportunities, and occupations of women in the late 1800s and early 1900s (see Appendix A).

When teachers design a unit collaboratively, an activity is planned and the guidesheets or supplementary materials created at the same time. The curriculum designers write a description of the activity as the motivation statement and refer the reader to the appendix that lists a model of the graphic. For example, Figure 6.1 models the graphic referred to in the motivation statement.

A guidesheet for this project could divide the questions into categories to help students organize the project and ensure some consistency of the information gathered from the different groups of interviewers. Students are still free to select issues within the interview but the guidesheet identifies key points and clarifies the purpose and the outcome of the activity.

Guidesheets are valuable organizational tools. They permit the teacher to guide an assignment while allowing students creative freedom. Creativity involves risk taking. All students have creativity to some degree, but feel more comfortable making decisions when given a model that clarifies expectations. Such a model is shown in Figure 6.2.

FIGURE 6.1

KWL Chart		
What We Know	**What We Want to Know**	**What We Have Learned**

FIGURE 6.2

Interview Guidesheet

Interviewers _____   Interview Subject _____

_____   Interview Date _____

_____   Interview Place _____

In this activity, you will develop a series of questions and conduct an interview to find out how the family roles, educational opportunities, and occupations of women have changed from the late 1800s and early 1900s to today. After gathering the information, be prepared to discuss the following three issues.

1. *Background Information.*   Who was your subject and how were his or her opinions formed? Roles could be different in different parts of the country, different settings (rural, urban, or suburban), or in different socioeconomic groups. Was the subject told stories by a mother or grandmother or does the information come from personal experiences? Background information helps you to understand the information shared.

2. *Personal History.*   What personal experiences has the subject had that show differences in attitudes and opportunities between the past and the present? How did the subject cope with these experiences? Was this behavior accepted or rejected by the members of the community and the family? In this section you will want to explore the experiences of the subject, stories shared by relatives, and the subjects' interpretations or attitudes about the issues discussed.

3. *Conclusions.*   What conclusions can your group draw about the roles of women in the past? How have attitudes and opportunities changed? Would it have been difficult to have attitudes or ambitions that were not consistent with accepted views of roles in the family and in society?

Care must be taken in designing a guidesheet. Teachers must make decisions about how much support to provide. If too much support is provided, students will simply copy the model and creativity is destroyed. In preparing a guidesheet, the teacher describes the assignment, clarifies the way the project will be used, and formulates questions to stimulate critical thinking. Freedom is provided within a set of parameters for individual creativity. As growth is achieved, support is gradually withdrawn and students are led to independence.

Since the authors are modeling the creation of the procedure section, a sample appendix section that includes the guidesheets for the activities is included. Note that activities with guidesheets contain a reference for the reader as to location of the supplementary materials.

THE PROCEDURE AND APPENDIX

After your group has gathered the content information, listed the concepts on the fact sheet, and planned the motivational activity, you are ready to write the procedures. The procedures are stated as succinctly as possible without distorting the meaning. Then they are labeled and sequenced in the order in which they will be taught. If the procedure includes a graphic organizer, note in the procedure section that an example of the organizer appears in the appendix.

It may be necessary at this point in the creative process to add or delete information listed on the fact sheet, so your group may want to assign classmates to specific roles. The researcher may search for additional content to support the activities. The drafter works with the designer of the graphics to be entered in the appendix. The computer specialist and the editor complete the word processing and check the plan to be sure it is consistent with the required format.

The following pages represent the author's model of a procedure section with appendixes.

PROCEDURE

Oral Reporting

Students share the results of their interviews and decide how the opportunities, education, and occupations of women in the late 1800s and early 1900s differ from the opportunities, education, and occupations of women today. Conclusions are listed on a chart (see Appendix B).

Research Readiness

Working in small groups, students are given a list of the names and occupations of famous Women of Achievement and asked to select a research subject.

Reading Comprehension

Biographies are distributed and students read in dyads to find the information suggested on a guidesheet (see Appendix C).

Sequencing Activity

Using newspaper print and magic markers, students create a timeline of their subject's life. The literature synopsis is used as the informational source.

Creative Writing

Students write a short paper using the guided reading responses and the timeline as background information for the creative writing project. In the paper, students describe how their subject's life would be different if she lived today.

Historical Event Project

Using *My Great Book of Discovery and Invention* and *The New York Public Library Book of Chronologies,* students select a historical event and plan a presentation for the class (see Appendix D).

Paraphrasing, Synthesizing, and Classifying Information

Using the historical research and information from the timeline as the information base, students construct a step book that identifies five major events in their subject's life (see Appendix E).

Technology Project

Using *My Great Book of Discovery and Invention,* the biography, and *The New York Public Library Book of Chronologies,* students select and research an invention that would have affected their subject's life. A fact sheet is designed to display major concepts suggested on the guidesheet. A real object is used to demonstrate the scientific principle that causes the invention to work (see Appendix F).

Exhibit

For the culminating activity, each group of students will create an exhibit with realia and posters that focus on their woman of achievement. Oral biographies, demonstrations of the inventions, and step books will be shared with students in other classrooms.

APPENDIX A

KWL CHART

What We Know	What We Want to Know	What We Have Learned

APPENDIX B

ROLES OF WOMEN YESTERDAY AND TODAY

	Women of Yesterday	Women of Today
Opportunities		
Education		
Occupations		

APPENDIX C

GUIDED READING

Team Members: **Date:** _____

_____   **Subject:** _____

_____   **Occupation:** _____

_____

_____

Read the biography to find the following information:

1. How was the childhood of your subject different from most women of this period?

2. How was your subject educated and what hardships did she have during this period of her life? Who encouraged her?

3. How was she different from other women?

4. What were her achievements and how did she change the period she lived in?

APPENDIX D

HISTORICAL EVENT GUIDESHEET

Historical events (disasters, plagues, wars) can greatly affect national attitudes, values, court decisions, and constitutional amendments. In the period from 1860 to 1920, many changes occurred in the public's attitude toward women and their place in society. These changes were very difficult for some to accept in the workplace and in positions of influence. Using the materials provided, identify one event that would have affected the life of your woman of achievement and plan a presentation for the class. Your information should come from more than one source.

Introduction

This section gives the reader the background information that is needed to understand the paper. It is written factually using references to support statements.

1. What factors led to the event?

2. When did the event occur and who was involved?

3. Could some precautions have been taken to prevent the event from happening?

Body

In this section, explain how this event may have influenced the life and attitudes of your woman of achievement and her family. The text may be written from your point of view but should be consistent with information found in the biography. Use the following questions to guide your conclusions.

1. How did the event affect your subject's life?

2. Was her reaction consistent with the attitudes of others in the community?

3. Did she take an active role in the solution of the problem that caused the event?

4. Was her life changed in any way as the result of the event?

Bibliography

List the sources of your information.

Delegation of Responsibilities

Explain how your group delegated the work among the team members.

APPENDIX D *(continued)*

LIBRARY RESEARCH GUIDESHEET

Team Members: **Due Date:** _____

_____   **Research Subject:** _____

_____   **Event:** _____

_____

_____

1. Describe the event that affected the life of your subject.

2. How did the event affect your subject and her family?

3. What were the sources of your information?

4. How did your group delegate the responsibilities?

5. How will you share the information with the class?

   Prepare an oral report   _____   Write a newspaper article   _____

   Conduct a panel discussion   _____   Construct a story board   _____

   Give a news radio report   _____   Create a video   _____

   Present a play   _____

APPENDIX D *(continued)*

HISTORICAL EVENT GRADING CRITERIA

Team Members: **Date:** _____

_____   **Section:** _____

_____

_____

_____

Introduction

Reflects accurate facts.   (8) _____
Reflects adequate research.

Body

Provides logical linkages with biographical subject.   (4) _____
Draws logical conclusions.   (4) _____

Bibliography

Multiple sources are identified.   (2) _____

Delegation of Responsibilities

Work is distributed fairly.   (2) _____

Total   (20) _____

Comments

APPENDIX E

THE STEP BOOK

A step book is a project that illustrates the facts of a story in five related categories. Amelia Earhart's biography could be divided into the following five categories:

1. Amelia's childhood
2. Learning to fly
3. Life as a Boston social worker
4. The disappearance
5. Amelia's contributions

Each page of a five-page booklet summarizes and illustrates one important concept in the life of your subject. Follow these steps to complete the project:

1. Take five sheets of 8-½" × 11" construction paper and make a hot dog fold on the first sheet 1-½" from the top. The fold is made on the second sheet 2" from the top, 2-½" from the top on the third sheet, 3" on the fourth sheet, and 3-½" on the fifth sheet.
2. Pages are placed inside one another along the folded edge to form a booklet.
3. Titles of each of the five stories are listed on the outside narrow flaps.
4. A separate story is written and illustrated on each of the five large pages.
5. The book is stapled together along the fold line after it has been written, illustrated, and laminated.

APPENDIX F

TECHNOLOGY PROJECT GUIDESHEET

Team Members: **Due Date:** _____

_____   **Research Subject:** _____

_____   **Invention:** _____

_____   **Inventor:** _____

_____

Select an Invention

Inventions can change the course of history. Using the information from your biography, *The New York Public Library Book of Chronologies,* and *My Great Book of Discovery and Invention,* select an invention that would have affected the life of your subject.

Research the Topic

Using information from a variety of sources, locate the historical background for your invention.

Who was the inventor? _____

When was the technology invented? _____

What was the inventor's motivation for creating the invention? _____

_____

How was the technology invented? _____

_____

Create a Fact Sheet on Posterboard or Newspaper Print

Create a fact sheet that explains the scientific concept and forces behind your invention.

Demonstrate the Scientific Concept Linked to Your Invention

Use a model or real object to demonstrate your invention.

Identify the Sources of Your Information _____

_____

Delegation of Responsibility

Describe how your group delegated responsibility for the assignment.

APPENDIX F *(continued)*

TECHNOLOGY PROJECT GRADING CRITERIA

Team Members:

_____

_____

_____

_____

Due Date: _____

Research Subject: _____

Invention: _____

Inventor: _____

Historical Background

Key issues are identified.   (3) _____
Issues are presented logically.   (3) _____

Fact Sheet

Facts are presented neatly.   (3) _____
Information presented is accurate.   (3) _____

Demonstration

The demonstration is well planned.   (3) _____

Informational Sources

Informational sources are identified.   (2) _____

Delegation of Responsibilities

Work is distributed fairly.   (3) _____

Total   (20) _____

Comments

CLOSURE STATEMENT

All students want to be successful. The role of the teacher is to lead pupils from dependent to independent learning. This takes careful planning, appropriately sequenced activities, and clear directions. Since some students have difficulty retaining a sequence of instructions at once, guidesheets provide a clear pathway to the successful completion of a project. Guidesheets also provide parameters and clarify the instructor's expectations while allowing freedom for individual creativity.

There is no substitute for planning. Many times teachers will have to think on their feet and modify the instruction because of student responses to an activity. However, the teacher who has carefully planned the curriculum is able to respond more smoothly in these situations. Planning curriculum and observing students' responses to the instruction is one of the most creative and challenging aspects of teaching.

REFERENCES

North, P. (1991). *My great big book of discovery and invention.* London: Bracken Books.
Wetterau, B. (1990). *The New York Public Library book of chronologies.* New York: Macmillan.

CHAPTER

ASSESSMENT, INTEGRATION STATEMENT, AND MATERIALS

Chapter 7 identifies the teacher's role in assessing and reporting accurate judgments of student progress. Objectives are described, tracking instruments are provided, and the connections between objectives and evaluation statements are clarified. Instruction is provided for the writing of the integration statement and the materials section of the unit plan.

The issue of school assessment is very political and can incite strong emotions in the public. To be prepared to clearly discuss the goals of our programs, as teachers, we must recognize the importance of assessment and the underlying cause of these emotional reactions. We also must be diligent in determining that the instruments we select, the methods we use, and the information we discuss is fair, accurate, current, and unbiased.

■ What safeguards must be taken to ensure that our judgments about students are accurate?

Assessment, Integration Statement, and Materials

Political Implications of Assessment	Assessment Defined	Performance Objectives	The Integration Statement
	■ Standardized Testing ■ Observation of Learning Behaviors ■ Normed and Criterion-Referenced Data	■ Content versus Performance Objectives ■ Mastery Objectives ■ Tracking Instruments for Mastery Objectives ■ Developmental Objectives ■ Tracking Instruments for Developmental Objectives ■ Evaluation Statements	■ Purpose of the Integration Statement ■ Format of the Integration Statement

POLITICAL IMPLICATIONS OF ASSESSMENT

Assessment is a very important function in the educational process. It is important not only to the teacher, but to the school administration, parents, publishing companies, the media, community, and the state and federal government. All of these individuals and groups need to make decisions that affect students, instruction, and school policy and can only be effective if based on accurate information provided by teachers. School data is being used to make many decisions, but the information is being used in different ways for different purposes, as shown in Figure 7.1.

For these reasons, it is very important that judgments made about students and school performance are accurate, unbiased, and collected from many sources over time. Teachers need to know how to design assessment instruments, administer tests, track performance, and discuss performance with parents. It is not enough to understand the results of assessment; teachers must also know what information is appropriate to share and what data should be kept confidential. Assessment is an important function of teaching and it is also very political.

FIGURE 7.1

How Is Educational Data Used?

Person or Group Interested	Type of Information	Decisions Made from the Data
Parents	Grouped and individual	Should we get a tutor? Should we save money for college? Are we living in a good school district?
School Administrators	Grouped	How is our school doing in comparison with other districts? Should the curriculum be revised?
Grant Funding Agencies	Grouped	Was the project successful?
Teachers	Grouped and individual	Is the level of instruction appropriate? Should I reteach the concept? How is John achieving? Should I refer Mary for special help?
Politicians	Grouped	What districts are in the greatest need of financial support?

ASSESSMENT DEFINED

The term *assessment* is not synonymous with testing. Assessment is a global term implying that judgments about student performance are based on test results as well as observation of classroom learning behaviors.

Standardized Testing

Standardized testing tells us how a student is performing on a given day (a snapshot of performance that can be used as a baseline). This information compares the child's achievement to the achievement of students in the norming population. Results of a class, school district, or a state can easily be grouped. Grouped information becomes important when districts are competing for government or grant funds, reporting progress to the public, or evaluating the effectiveness of curriculum materials. An example of a standardized test that all college students are familiar with is the SAT.

Observation of Learning Behaviors

Observational methods track individual growth over time. A child's achievement is compared with his past performance using a rubric or standard as the criterion. Rubrics can be published but they are often developed by teachers and are an outgrowth of the curriculum.

Teachers have a wealth of information available that can be used for informal assessment—informal reading inventories, homework assignments, creative writing assignments, responses to questions, projects, reports, and cloze procedures. All of these activities can be used for assessment purposes when rubrics are developed to measure growth and status sheets track changes in learning behaviors. In elementary school, children are taught cursive writing using a published style sheet. The style sheet (for example—PO Peterson) is the criterion that is used to judge a student's growth in writing.

Normed and Criterion-Referenced Data

Both normed (resulting from standardized tests) and criterion-referenced (comparing individual achievement against a standard) information are important components of the assessment process. If the data from both sources agree, we can be comfortable that our judgments are correct. If a student does well on homework papers, teacher-made tests, group work, and class projects, he is showing us that he understands the concepts taught. That student should also do well on the standardized exam.

When the data disagree, the teacher needs to find out why. It could be that the standardized test does not measure what was taught or that the student was not well on the day of the test resulting in an invalid score. Assessment not only tells us about students, it also provides the stimulus for reflection, curriculum revision, selection of materials, and self-evaluation.

Teachers need data not only to make judgments about student progress, but also to make decisions about the effectiveness of their teaching, the appropriateness of the content depth, the choice of instructional materials, and the validity/reliability of the evaluation instruments and methods. Good assessment is an outgrowth of the instruction and is a combination of both formal and informal measures.

PERFORMANCE OBJECTIVES

Effective teaching is not magic. Sometimes the results can seem magical and those moments are the reason why many of us chose a teaching career, cherishing our profession above all other career paths. The effective teacher can be described as an experimenter or a scientist in human behavior. Effective teaching involves fact finding, careful planning, skillful teaching, observation of student behavior, reflection and self-assessment, and curriculum revision. Teachers modify and adapt materials to fit the skill levels, attention spans, ages, and interests of the students in the classroom. To do this well, teachers must be clear about students' backgrounds, parental expectations, district philosophy, and state curriculum standards. This information is used in the development of performance objectives.

Content versus Performance Objectives

Marzano and Kendall (1995) describe content objectives as standards that describe learning in terms of knowledge and skills to be acquired. Performance objectives are written in terms of tasks performed by students that demonstrate knowledge and skills. Content objectives focus on the specific content taught; performance objectives presume that knowledge or skill is defined by embedding it in a task. With a performance objective, students must demonstrate that they are able to apply the knowledge. Performance objectives also put knowledge in a specific context (for example, in an oral report or an essay).

Content Objective

The student demonstrates understanding of the concept of time.

Performance Objective

1.0 understands the concept of time
    1.1 reads numbers correctly
    1.2 masters the concept of before and after
    1.3 counts by fives
    1.4 distinguishes between purposes of hour and minute hands

---

Marzano and Kendall believe that performance standards are a critical component of a standards-based approach to schooling and that performance and content standards can be used effectively together.

Performance objectives fall into two categories: mastery objectives and developmental objectives. Performance objectives are useful in the design of informal assessment instruments such as teacher-made tests, rubrics, and grading criteria.

If we are to design curricula, we must have a clear understanding of what children know and what we want them to achieve. This organization empowers us to make choices about the most effective material, methodology, and strategies for the children under our supervision. Performance objectives also help us to recognize individual differences and communicate the purpose of the instruction to others.

Performance objectives are stated in terms of learning experiences and learning outcomes. The learning experience identifies the process taught and the learning outcomes list the products of the instruction. The learning outcomes all begin with verbs.

1.0 Study of the alphabet   (*Learning Experience*)
    1.1 Names letters in sequence   (*Learning Outcomes*)
    1.2 Names letters out of sequence
    1.3 Associates the sound with the consonant
    1.4 Associates the sound with verb
    1.5 Sounds out simple words
    1.6 Creates simple words

The number 1.0 identifies the first learning experience; 1.1 indicates the first learning outcome. Objectives for the Women of Achievement Unit could assess students' ability to research.

1.0 Researches effectively
    1.1 Identifies research topic
    1.2 Locates relevant material
    1.3 Records source of information accurately
    1.4 Selects an interesting reporting format
    1.5 Reports information accurately

Mastery Objectives

The mastery objectives involve simple content or skills that teachers expect children to achieve during the school year. If students are not able to demonstrate that they can complete the outcomes independently, additional support or instruction should be provided. Mastery objectives involve the outcomes of the tasks that the teacher identifies as skills, content, or processes that make up the curriculum for the school year and the grade level taught. Learning outcomes are written by identifying and sequencing the behaviors that students demonstrate based on their depth of understanding. You will recall in Chapter 3 we recommended that the teacher identify annual goals. The annual goals are developed at the beginning of each year and used to design performance objectives.

Skills	Content	Processes
Study of Alphabet	Story Telling	Listening
Competency with Numbers 1–100	Oral Reading of Literature	Verbalization of Thoughts

Tracking Instruments for Mastery Objectives

During the day teachers make many observations of students' learning behaviors. However, with twenty-five to thirty students to teach, these observations would soon be difficult to recall accurately without some kind of a tracking system. It is also true that we cannot be sure learning has taken place until the behavior is repeated several times. A student can respond positively to the instruction one day, and become confused by the next. A tracking instrument enables us to look for patterns of behavior objectively over time.

Mastery objectives can be tracked on a class status sheet developed by the teacher. It is easy to construct, takes little classroom time to use, and can be useful in reporting academic progress to parents during a conference. Tracking instruments are placed in the appendix sections of the unit plan.

Figure 7.2 shows an example of a classroom status sheet. Use the code in the key to track mastery of the learning outcomes and date the observations. Once the information is gathered, it can be used to guide decisions about mini-lessons and reinforcement activities. Teachers may also want to group children for direct instruction in the skill needing additional practice. You may want to use a different coding system to record performance, but it should be kept simple and easy to record.

Developmental Objectives

Developmental objectives involve complex learning outcomes based on levels of cognition (critical thinking, reasoning, problem solving), and learning often spans across grade levels. An example is telling time. If you ask teachers if they teach an

FIGURE 7.2

Classroom Status Sheet

Student	Names Letters in Sequence	Names Letters out of Sequence	Associates Sound with Consonant	Associates Sound with Verb	Sounds Out Simple Words	Creates Simple Words
Mary						
Tom						
Trent						

Key   D = developing
N = not evident
M = mastery

element of time in first grade they will agree, but since students master abstraction at different stages, some students will still be learning to tell time in fourth grade. By fourth grade, all students would be expected to demonstrate competence. Teachers at earlier grade levels know that they will introduce time concepts because the instruction builds the background of experience that is necessary to master the task. Developmental objectives track complex learning outcomes across grade levels.

To begin the construction of developmental objectives, it is best to start with a simple framework. After identifying your learning experience, create one knowledge outcome, one understanding outcome, and one application outcome.

2.0 Reading
    2.1 Knows new vocabulary   (knowledge)
    2.2 Paraphrases plot accurately   (understanding)
    2.3 Applies information read to new situation   (application)

3.0 Writing
    3.1 Demonstrates appropriate grammar skills (knowledge)
    3.2 Expresses thoughts in a logical sequence (understanding)
    3.3 Writes for a specific purpose   (application)

When you begin to use the rubric with students, you may wish to insert additional learning outcomes. This is perfectly appropriate. Rubrics are perfected through the revision process. However, it is important to keep learning outcomes content-free so that the completed rubrics can be used with all units of study. Examples of expanded outcomes are included on the tracking instrument for the developmental objectives.

Tracking Instruments for Developmental Objectives

Developmental objectives cross grade levels, so an individual status sheet for each student must be designed by the teachers who will be involved in tracking the data. The school principal should also be involved because it may be necessary to reschedule planning periods or explain the process or results to parents. The status sheets follow the students through elementary school and are compared with baseline formal testing results. Figure 7.3 is an example of an individual status sheet.

Mastery objectives are appropriate for content that can be expressed and evaluated through observation of a sequence of skills. Developmental objectives are used when the learning involves cognitive processes. We believe that instruction should be balanced and the type of objective written is determined by the content taught. Objectives developed, rubrics created, and the tracking instruments used should be reviewed and revised periodically after collecting and reporting student information.

FIGURE 7.3

Individual Status Sheet: Reading and Writing Record

Student Trent Jones

Outcomes	Grade 3		Grade 4		Grade 5		Grade 6	
Date	9/95	5/96	9/96	5/97	9/97	5/98	9/98	5/99
Reading								
Masters new vocabulary								
Responds correctly to questions								
Paraphrases accurately								
Summarizes effectively								
Applies information to new situations								
Writing								
Identifies topic independently								
Demonstrates appropriate grammar skills								
Demonstrates understanding of mechanics								
Uses vivid language								
Expresses thoughts in logical sequence								
Writes for a specific purpose								
Instructor								

Key C = consistently
O = occasionally
N = not evident

EVALUATION STATEMENTS

Creating a unit plan is a creative process that involves thinking about curriculum as a whole and also in sequential parts. In effect, the process is a Gestalt.

The planning wheel provides an overview. The fact sheet identifies specific concepts that are expanded and sequenced into the procedure section. All of the procedures are important because they link subject matter and make it more interesting and memorable for students by developing schema. However, after the procedures are written, the task involves selecting the most important skills, content, or processes that will be developed into unit objectives. This decision is made by referring back to the annual goals. Using the goals as a guide, you will prioritize the procedures and select the learning experiences that will be the major focus of the instruction.

The evaluation statements must be directly related to the performance objectives. They are the major focus of the unit plan and it is the responsibility of the teacher to identify students who demonstrate mastery and those who will need additional guided practice. Evaluation statements are not activities but a rewording of the performance objectives.

Performance Objectives

1.0 Library Research
    1.1 Identifies research topic
    1.2 Locates relevant material
    1.3 Records the source of the material accurately
    1.4 Selects an interesting reporting format
    1.5 Reports information accurately
2.0 Reading
    2.1 Masters new vocabulary
    2.2 Responds correctly to questions
    2.3 Paraphrases accurately
    2.4 Summarizes effectively
    2.5 Applies information to new situations
3.0 Writing
    3.1 Identifies topic independently
    3.2 Demonstrates appropriate grammar skills
    3.3 Demonstrates understanding of mechanics
    3.4 Uses vivid language
    3.5 Expresses thoughts in logical sequence
    3.6 Writes for a specific purpose

Evaluation Statements

1.0 Students will demonstrate mastery of Objective 1 by identifying a research topic, locating relevant material, recording the source of the materials, selecting an interesting reporting format, and reporting information accurately.
2.0 Students will demonstrate mastery of Objective 2 by knowing new vocabulary, responding correctly to questions, paraphrasing content, summarizing concepts, and applying information read to a new situation.
3.0 Students will demonstrate mastery of Objective 3 by identifying a topic independently, demonstrating appropriate grammar skills, demonstrating understanding of appropriate mechanics, using vivid language, expressing thoughts in logical sequence, and writing for a specific purpose.

THE INTEGRATION STATEMENT AND MATERIALS

The Purpose of the Integration Statement

The integration statement is a narrative overview of the unit plan. It informs teachers of the skills, content, and processes included in the instruction. This information is gathered by reviewing the activities listed in the procedure section and the planning wheel. It is a summary of the instruction that allows instructors to decide quickly if the curriculum is appropriate for their class.

Format for the Integration Statement

The integration statement for the American Women of Achievement unit plan is written in the following format.

> In this unit plan, students will apply reading, language arts, science, social studies, mathematics, geographic, and physics concepts to the biography of a Woman of Achievement who lived in the period between 1860 and 1920. Also reinforced are skills and processes in comprehension, library research, creative writing, paraphrasing, summarizing, and oral reporting.

Materials

In this section, list the materials that will be used in the unit plan.

CLOSURE STATEMENT

Mastery and developmental objectives enable teachers to integrate assessment with curriculum. Status sheets are a needs assessment that empowers teachers to identify students who are having difficulty so that individual instruction can be provided. Unclear concepts can be retaught to the students needing additional support, while advanced children apply concepts to new situations. Instruction is no longer generic.

REFERENCES

Linn, R. L., & Gronlund, N. E. (1995). *Measurement and assessment in teaching* (7th ed.). Englewood Cliffs, NJ: Merrill.

Marzano, R. J., & Kendall, J. S. (1995). The McRel database: A tool for constructing local standards. *Educational Leadership, 52*(6), 42–47.

CHAPTER

8

THE SAMPLE UNIT PLAN: AMELIA EARHART: AMERICAN WOMAN OF ACHIEVEMENT

LITERATURE CONCEPT

Amelia Earhart was a risk taker who defied the conventions of her era to become a role model for women who wanted careers in male-oriented occupations. Why did Amelia become a hero to the American public when so many other nontraditional women were criticized and rejected?

INTEGRATION STATEMENT

In this unit plan, students will apply reading, language arts, science, social studies, mathematics, geography, and physics concepts to the biography of a Woman of Achievement who lived in the period between 1860 and 1920. Also reinforced are skills and processes in comprehension, library research, creative writing, paraphrasing, summarizing, and oral reporting.

OBJECTIVES

1.0 Library Research
    1.1 Identifies research topic
    1.2 Locates relevant material
    1.3 Records the source of the material accurately
    1.4 Selects an interesting reporting format
    1.5 Reports information accurately

2.0 Reading
    2.1 Masters new vocabulary
    2.2 Responds correctly to questions
    2.3 Paraphrases accurately
    2.4 Summarizes effectively
    2.5 Applies information read to new situations

3.0 Writing
    3.1 Identifies topic independently
    3.2 Demonstrates appropriate grammar skills
    3.3 Demonstrates understanding of mechanics
    3.4 Uses vivid language
    3.5 Expresses thoughts in logical sequence
    3.6 Writes for a specific purpose

MATERIALS

(1) Biography for every four students
     Magic markers
(1) Roll of newsprint
     My Great Book of Discovery and Invention

MOTIVATION

After completing a KWL chart, students will develop a series of questions to ask retirement home residents about family roles, educational opportunities, and occupations of women in the late 1800s and early 1900s (see Appendix A).

PROCEDURE

Oral Reporting

Students share the results of their interviews and decide how the opportunities, education, and occupations of women in the late 1800s and early 1900s differ from the opportunities, education, and occupations of women today. Conclusions are listed on a chart (see Appendix B).

Research Readiness

Working in small groups, students are given a list of the names and occupations of famous Women of Achievement and asked to select a research subject.

Reading Comprehension

Biographies are distributed and students read in dyads to find the information suggested on a guidesheet (see Appendix C).

Sequencing Activity

Using newspaper print and magic markers, students create a timeline of their subject's life. The literature synopsis is used as the informational source.

Creative Writing

Students write a short paper using the guided reading responses and the timeline as background information for the creative writing project. In the paper, students describe how their subject's life would be different if she lived today.

Historical Event Project

Using *My Great Book of Discovery and Invention* and *The New York Public Library Book of Chronologies,* students select a historical event and plan a presentation for the class (see Appendix D).

Paraphrasing, Synthesizing, and Classifying Information

Using the historical research and information from the timeline as the information base, students construct a step book that identifies five major events in their subject's life (see Appendix E).

Technology Project

Using *My Great Book of Discovery and Invention,* the biography, and *The New York Public Library Book of Chronologies,* students select and research an invention that would have affected their subject's life. A fact sheet is designed to display major concepts suggested on the guidesheet. A real object is used to demonstrate the scientific principle that causes the invention to work (see Appendix F).

Exhibit

For the culminating activity, each group of students will create an exhibit with realia and posters that focus on their woman of achievement. Oral biographies, demonstrations of the inventions, and step books will be shared with students in other classrooms.

AMELIA EARHART FACT SHEET

Social Studies

HISTORY OF FLIGHT

1200s   The Chinese used kites to spy on their enemies.

1738   Daniel Bernoulli discovered the airfoil. The principle behind the airfoil was that the increasing movement of a gas or liquid lowers its pressure.

1783   Montgolfier invented the first hot-air balloon designed to carry passengers. The French balloon carried its passengers five miles on the initial flight.

1783   Shortly after Montgolfier's flight, Jacques Charles successfully piloted the first hydrogen balloon.

1849   Sir George Cayley flew a child in the first glider. Four years later, Cayley's coachman became the first adult glider passenger and, upon landing, resigned his job.

1852   French engineer Henri Giffard invented the first steam-powered airship.

1903   The Wright brothers flew the first powered airplane at Kitty Hawk, North Carolina.

1907   The first gasoline powered helicopter took flight in France. The helicopter was invented by Paul Cornu. It took about 30 years to perfect a reliable helicopter.

1908   Glenn Hammond Curtiss, an American inventor and aviation pioneer, made the first public flights in the United States. He also established the first flying school in 1909 and made a breathtaking flight from Albany to New York City.

1909   Louis Bl'eriot, a French aviator and inventor, was the first aviator to cross the English Channel in a heavier-than-air machine.

1911   Glenn Hammond Curtiss invented ailerons and, after World War I, made radical advances in the design of planes and their motors.

1922   Anton Herman Gerard was a German-American aircraft manufacturer who owned factories in Germany that produced the triplanes and bi-planes used in World War I. An inventor who developed the mechanism that allowed machine-gun bullets to be fired through a rotating propeller without hitting the blades, Gerard also developed the first commercial aircraft.

Science

WEATHER INSTRUMENTS

Meteorology   Meteorology is the science that studies atmospheric patterns and weather.

(continued)

Forecast	Forecast is a future prediction of the weather based on observation and analysis of atmospheric conditions. The forecast describes what is most likely to happen. Meteorologists (scientists who study weather) make these predictions by measuring wind temperature, air pressure, wind speed, and wind direction.
Weather vane	A weather vane is a movable device attached to a pole that shows wind direction.
Anemometer	An anemometer measures wind speed. Cups catch the wind making the anemometer's arms spin. As the arms spin, the wind speed can be measured.
Wind sock	A wind sock shows both wind speed and wind direction. It looks like a cloth cone open at both ends. The wind sock twists on a pole showing the direction of the wind. If the sock is blowing straight out, it shows the wind is blowing strongly. If the sock is limp, there is little wind.
Relative humidity	Relative humidity is the amount of water vapor in the air compared to the greatest amount of water vapor the air can hold at that temperature. Warm air can hold more water vapor than cold air. Relative humidity is stated as a percent and is measured with a wet and dry bulb thermometer.

WEATHER FORECASTS

Air mass	An air mass is a large body of air extending hundreds or thousands of miles horizontally and sometimes as high as the stratosphere. An air mass has the same amount of moisture and humidity throughout. The weather in a certain area of land is determined by the air mass. Changes in the weather occur when air masses move.
Front	A front is the boundary between two air masses that are not alike. When cold air moves into a warmer air mass, it is called a cold front.
Jet streams	Jet streams are high speed ribbons of air that influence the movement of air masses. Jet streams move from west to east or from north to south in a wavelike motion.

WEATHER MAP

Isotherm	An isotherm is a line drawn on a weather map connecting areas that have the same temperature.
Isobar	An isobar is a line drawn on a weather map connecting areas that have the same air pressure. Air pressure is given in units called millibars. An area of high pressure brings fair weather; low pressure brings cloudy weather.

(continued)

(continued)

STORMS

Thunderstorm   Thunderstorms are caused by rapidly rising updrafts of warm air that contain large amounts of water vapor. Condensation occurs as the warm air rises and cools causing the water vapor to crystalize and form a cloud. A cool air current (downdraft) causes the moisture to fall to the earth in the form of rain or hail.

Tornado   A tornado is a violent, destructive whirling wind accompanied by a funnel-shaped cloud that travels in a narrow path over the land. No one knows exactly what causes tornadoes. In a tornado, a layer of warm humid air close to the ground becomes trapped by a layer of cold, dry air above it. Then, a rapidly moving cold front moves into the region. The cold front lifts the warm air between the two layers of cold air. The warm air breaks through the cold air and rushes upward in the form of a twisting mass called the tornado funnel.

Hurricane   A hurricane is a violent storm that develops over the ocean in a tropical area. Hurricanes are usually accompanied by rains, thunder, lightning, and winds up to 74 miles per hour. Hurricanes contain a rotating mass of air with a low pressure center. Each hurricane has a calm region in the center called the eye of the storm. The strongest winds of the hurricane rotate around the eye.

PHYSICS

Flight   Balloons and airships are heavier than air and fly by generating a force that overcomes their weight and supports them in the air. Kites use the power of wind to keep them aloft. All winged aircraft, including gliders and helicopters, make use of the airfoil and its lifting power. Vertical takeoff aircraft direct the power of their jet engines downward and heave themselves off the ground by brute force.

   The two principles that govern heavier-than-air flight are the same as those that propel powered vessels—action and reaction, and suction. When applied to flight, suction is known as lift.

Airfoil   The cross-section of a wing has a shape called airfoil. As the wing moves through the air, the air divides to pass around the wing. The airfoil is curved so that air passing above the wing moves faster than the air passing beneath. Fast-moving air has a lower pressure than slow-moving air. The pressure of the air is therefore greater beneath the wing than above it. This difference in air pressure forces the wing upward. The force is called lift.

APPENDIX A

KWL CHART

What We Know	What We Want to Know	What We Have Learned

APPENDIX B

ROLES OF WOMEN YESTERDAY AND TODAY

	Women of Yesterday	Women of Today
Opportunities		
Education		
Occupations		

APPENDIX C

GUIDED READING

Team Members: **Date:** _____

_____   **Subject:** _____

_____   **Occupation:** _____

_____

_____

Read the biography to find the following information:

1. How was the childhood of your subject different from most women of this period?

2. How was your subject educated and what hardships did she have during this period of her life? Who encouraged her?

3. How was she different from other women?

4. What were her achievements and how did she change the period she lived in?

APPENDIX D

HISTORICAL EVENT GUIDESHEET

Historical events (disasters, plagues, wars) can greatly affect national attitudes, values, court decisions, and constitutional amendments. In the period from 1860 to 1920, many changes occurred in the public's attitude toward women and their place in society. These changes were very difficult for some to accept in the workplace and in positions of influence. Using the materials provided, identify one event that would have affected the life of your woman of achievement and plan a presentation for the class. Your information should come from more than one source.

Introduction

This section gives the reader the background information that is needed to understand the paper. It is written factually using references to support statements.

1. What factors led to the event?

2. When did the event occur and who was involved?

3. Could some precautions have been taken to prevent the event from happening?

Body

In this section, explain how this event may have influenced the life and attitudes of your woman of achievement and her family. The text may be written from your point of view but should be consistent with information found in the biography. Use the following questions to guide your conclusions.

1. How did the event affect your subject's life?

2. Was her reaction consistent with the attitudes of others in the community?

3. Did she take an active role in the solution to the problem that caused the event?

4. Was her life changed in any way as the result of the event?

Bibliography

List the sources of your information.

Delegation of Responsibilities

Explain how your group delegated the work among the team members.

APPENDIX D *(continued)*

LIBRARY RESEARCH GUIDESHEET

Team Members: **Due Date:** _____

_____

                                           Research Subject: _____

_____

                                           Event: _____

_____

_____

1. Describe the event that affected the life of your subject.

2. How did the event affect your subject and her family?

3. What were the sources of your information?

4. How did your group delegate the responsibilities?

5. How will you share the information with the class?

   Prepare an oral report   _____   Write a newspaper article   _____

   Conduct a panel discussion   _____   Construct a story board   _____

   Give a news radio report   _____   Create a video   _____

   Present a play   _____

APPENDIX D *(continued)*

HISTORICAL EVENT GRADING CRITERIA

Team Members: **Date:** _____

_____   **Section:** _____

_____

_____

_____

Introduction

    Reflects accurate facts.   (8) _____
    Reflects adequate research.

Body

    Provides logical linkages with biographical subject.   (4) _____
    Draws logical conclusions.   (4) _____

Bibliography

    Multiple sources are identified.   (2) _____

Delegation of Responsibilities

    Work is distributed fairly.   (2) _____

Total   (20) _____

Comments

APPENDIX E

THE STEP BOOK

A step book is a project that illustrates the facts of a story in five related categories. Amelia Earhart's biography could be divided into the following five categories:

1. Amelia's childhood

2. Learning to fly

3. Life as a Boston social worker

4. The disappearance

5. Amelia's contributions

Each page of a 5-page booklet summarizes and illustrates one important concept in the life of your subject. Follow these steps to complete the project:

1. Take five sheets of 8-½" × 11" construction paper and make a hot dog fold on the first sheet 1-½" from the top. The fold is made on the second sheet 2" from the top, 2-½" from the top on the third sheet, 3" on the fourth sheet, and 3-½" on the fifth sheet.

2. Pages are placed inside one another along the folded edge to form a booklet.

3. Titles of each of the five stories are listed on the outside narrow flaps.

4. A separate story is written and illustrated on each of the five large pages.

5. The book is stapled together along the fold line after it has been written, illustrated, and laminated.

APPENDIX F

TECHNOLOGY PROJECT GUIDESHEET

Team Members: **Due Date:** _____

_____   **Research Subject:** _____

_____   **Invention:** _____

_____   **Inventor:** _____

_____

Select an Invention

Inventions can change the course of history. Using the information from your biography, *The New York Public Library Book of Chronologies,* and *My Great Book of Discovery and Invention,* select an invention that would have affected the life of your subject.

Research the Topic

Using information from a variety of sources, locate the information that provides the historical background for your invention.

Who was the inventor? _____

When was the technology invented? _____

What was the inventor's motivation for creating the invention? _____

_____

How was the technology invented? _____

_____

Create a Fact Sheet on Posterboard or Newspaper Print

Create a fact sheet that explains the scientific concept and forces behind your invention.

Demonstrate the Scientific Concept Linked to Your Invention

Use a model or real object to demonstrate your invention.

Identify the Sources of Your Information _____

_____

Delegation of Responsibility

Describe how your group delegated responsibility for the assignment.

APPENDIX F *(continued)*

TECHNOLOGY PROJECT GRADING CRITERIA

Team Members:
_____

_____

_____

_____

Due Date: _____

Research Subject: _____

Invention: _____

Inventor: _____

Historical Background

Key issues are identified.   (3) _____

Issues are presented logically.   (3) _____

Fact Sheet

Facts are presented neatly.   (3) _____

Information presented is accurate.   (3) _____

Demonstration

The demonstration is well planned.   (3) _____

Informational Sources

Informational sources are identified.   (2) _____

Delegation of Responsibilities

Work is distributed fairly.   (3) _____

Total   (20) _____

Comments

EVALUATION

1.0 Students will demonstrate mastery of Objective 1 by identifying a research topic, locating relevant material, recording the source of the materials, selecting an interesting reporting format, and reporting information accurately.

2.0 Students will demonstrate mastery of Objective 2 by knowing new vocabulary, responding correctly to questions, paraphrasing content, summarizing concepts, and applying information read to a new situation.

3.0 Students will demonstrate mastery of Objective 3 by identifying a topic independently, demonstrating appropriate grammar skills, demonstrating understanding of appropriate mechanics, using vivid language, expressing thoughts in logical sequence, and writing for a specific purpose.

BIBLIOGRAPHY

Barmeier, J. (1997). *Manners and customs.* New York: Chelsea House Publishers.

Ciment, J. (1995). *Law and order.* New York: Chelsea House Publishers.

Leuzzi, L. (1995). *Transportation.* New York: Chelsea House Publishers.

Leuzzi, L. (1995). *Urban life.* New York: Chelsea House Publishers.

North, P. (1991). *My great big book of discovery and invention.* London: Bracken Books.

Ritchie, D. (1996). *Frontier life.* New York: Chelsea House Publishers.

Ritchie, D., & Israel, F. (1995). *Health and medicine.* New York: Chelsea House Publishers.

Wetterau, B. (1990). *The New York Public Library book of chronologies.* New York: Prentice Hall Press.

DELEGATION OF RESPONSIBILITIES

This project was completed in partial fulfillment for the course, ELED 322: Teaching of Reading. Anne Mallery and Roger Wilson researched the content and the methodology. Roger served as researcher and typist. Anne Mallery designed the activities and edited the product.

CHAPTER 9

UNIT FRAMEWORK: NATIVE AMERICAN NATIONS

While there is question about the time that the first Indians reached the Americas, scientists believe that Native Americans are descendants of an early Mongoloid population that crossed a land bridge that existed from Siberia to Alaska from 26,000 to 8,000 B.C. The land corridor was 1,000 miles wide, free of trees, and arctic in climate. Because plants could not grow in this environment, the early travelers were hunters, gatherers, and fishermen. They must have lived in underground houses, worn fur clothing, and used fire to withstand the cold. These daring immigrants moved into North America, eastward into Alaska, and down the east side of the Rocky Mountains, spreading over large parts of the continent not covered by glaciers.

When Columbus discovered the New World, Native Americans occupied almost the entire landscape of North and South America and adjacent islands from Greenland to Tierra del Fuego. Adjustments to the climates, vegetation, and wildlife in the various geographic areas resulted in a broad spectrum of cultures. These cultures ranged from little family groups struggling to obtain a meager subsistence to the great civilizations of Mexico and Peru that had royal families, elaborate economic and political structures, complex technologies, and exquisite art forms. Researchers estimate that these groups had as many as 1,000 to 2,000 different languages and as many unique cultures.

Estimates of the Native American population in 1492 A.D. vary greatly. In addition, Native Americans had been isolated from the Old World for thousands of years and had no immunity to diseases of the Europeans, Africans, and Asians. Between 1530 and 1600, thirty-one epidemics swept across the Atlantic Coast from South America to Canada. These epidemics were so so disastrous the Native American population of North America fell from seven million to three million within one hundred years.

RELEVANCE OF THE THEME TO TEACHERS

Most classroom teachers hope to instill a respect for people of other cultures and the environment in their pupils. The theme of Native American Nations addresses both of these issues. As we examine the adaptation of people to their environment, we gain greater understanding of the customs, rituals, and values that shape behaviors. Insight into the roots of the beliefs of others helps students to better understand their own culture and become open to and accepting of the cultures of others.

HISTORICAL BACKGROUND

Even though the early Native Americans were different in many ways, they shared deeply rooted religious beliefs based on love of nature and respect for the earth. Each tribe had its own creation story that was in sharp contrast to the migration theory. Some tribes believed that they emerged from sacred, underground sites in the earth to populate the continent. One consistent theme among Native Americans was that the earth was first covered with water and living beings (mostly animals) and they brought mud from the bottom to form the earth. This all occurred before humans emerged from the underground. Other tribes believed that they were the offspring of divine beings or emerged from the sky.

The tribal civilizations were advanced in many ways. The Aztecs built magnificent pyramid-shaped temples, canals, bridges, ball courts, and complex cities. Most Aztecs bathed once a day, which contrasted sharply to the hygiene habits of Europeans at that time. The Mayans were also builders of pyramids and developed a calendar and mathematical systems.

Other tribes were successful farmers and developed food products that changed the eating habits of the world. Corn, white and sweet potatoes, squashes, pumpkins, tomatoes, strawberries, maple syrup, raspberries, cacao, and beans were all developed by Native American farmers. Indians also contributed to the field of medicine through the use of herbal remedies that provided relief for many common illnesses.

NATIVE AMERICAN NATIONS

RESEARCH TOPIC SIGN-UP SHEET

List the members of your group and your section with your research subject.

The Apache

_____

_____

_____

_____

The Blackfoot

_____

_____

_____

The Cherokee

_____

_____

_____

_____

The Cheyenne

_____

_____

_____

_____

The Chickasaw

_____

_____

_____

_____

(continued)

(continued)

The Chinook

_____

_____

_____

The Coast Salish Peoples

_____

_____

_____

The Hopi

_____

_____

_____

The Huron

_____

_____

_____

The Inuit

_____

_____

_____

The Iroquois

_____

_____

_____

_____

(continued)

The Kiowa

_____
_____
_____
_____

The Mohawk

_____
_____
_____
_____

The Narragansett

_____
_____
_____
_____

The Navajos

_____
_____
_____
_____

The Nez Perce

_____
_____
_____
_____

The Ojibwa

_____
_____
_____
_____

(continued)

(continued)

The Osage

_____

_____

_____

_____

The Paiute

_____

_____

_____

_____

The Powhatan Tribes

_____

_____

_____

_____

The Pueblo

_____

_____

_____

_____

The Sac and Fox

_____

_____

_____

_____

The Seminole

_____

_____

_____

_____

(continued)

The Shawnee

        _____

        _____

        _____

        _____

The Teton Sioux

        _____

        _____

        _____

        _____

The Wampanoag

        _____

        _____

        _____

The Zuni

        _____

        _____

        _____

NATIVE AMERICAN NATIONS

BIBLIOGRAPHY

Bonvillain, N. (1989). *The Huron.* Philadelphia: Chelsea House Publishers.
Bonvillain, N. (1992). *The Mohawk.* Philadelphia: Chelsea House Publishers.
Bonvillain, N. (1994a). *The Hopi.* Philadelphia: Chelsea House Publishers.
Bonvillain, N. (1994b). *The Teton Sioux.* Philadelphia: Chelsea House Publishers.
Bonvillain, N. (1995a). *The Inuit.* Philadelphia: Chelsea House Publishers.
Bonvillain, N. (1995b). *The Sac and Fox.* Philadelphia: Chelsea House Publishers.
Bonvillain, N. (1995c). *The Zuni.* Philadelphia: Chelsea House Publishers.
Bonvillain, N. (1996). *Native American religion.* Philadelphia: Chelsea House Publishers.
Bonvillain, N. (1997). *The Santee Sioux.* Philadelphia: Chelsea House Publishers.
Brown, F. (1997). *American Indian science: A new look at old cultures.* New York: Twenty-First
     Century Books.
Eagle/Walking Turtle. (1994). *Indian America.* Santa Fe, NM: John Muir Publications.
Feest, C. F. (1990). *The Pohatan tribes.* Philadelphia: Chelsea House Publishers.
Francis, L. (1995). *Native time: A historical time line of Native America.* New York: St. Martin's
     Press.
Franklin, R. J. (1990). *The Pauite.* Philadelphia: Chelsea House Publishers.
Garbarino, M. S. (1989). *The Seminole.* Philadelphia: Chelsea House Publishers.
Graymont, B. (1988). *The Iroquois.* Philadelphia: Chelsea House Publishers.
Green, M. D. (1990). *The Creeks.* Philadelphia: Chelsea House Publishers.
Green, R. (1992). *Women in American Indian society.* Philadelphia: Chelsea House Publishers.
Hale, D. K. (1991). *The Chickasaw.* Philadelphia: Chelsea House Publishers.
Hoig, S. (1984). *The Cheyenne.* Philadelphia: Chelsea House Publishers.
Iverson, P. (1990). *The Navajos.* Philadelphia: Chelsea House Publishers.
Kelly, L. C. (1990). *Federal Indian policy.* Philadelphia: Chelsea House Publishers.
Kopper, P. (1986). *The Smithsonian book of North American Indians before the coming of the
     Europeans.* New York: Smithsonian Books.
Lacey, T. J. (1995). *The Blackfeet.* Philadelphia: Chelsea House Publishers.
Lavender, D. S. (1989). *Let me be free: The Nez Perce tragedy.* Philadelphia: Chelsea House
     Publishers.
Liptak, K. (1990). *North American Indian medicine people.* Philadelphia: Chelsea House
     Publishers.
Liptak, K. (1992a). *North American Indian ceremonies.* Philadelphia: Chelsea House
     Publishers.
Liptak, K. (1992b). *North American Indian survival skills.* Philadelphia: Chelsea House
     Publishers.
Liptak, K. (1992c). *North American Indian tribal chiefs.* Philadelphia: Chelsea House
     Publishers.
Melody, M. E. (1989). *The Apache.* Philadelphia: Chelsea House Publishers.
Oritz, A. (1994). *The Pueblo.* Philadelphia: Chelsea House Publishers.
Perdue, T. (1989). *The Cherokee.* Philadelphia: Chelsea House Publishers.
Porter, F. W. (1989). *The Coast Salish People.* Philadelphia: Chelsea House Publishers.
Ritchie, D. (1996). *Frontier life.* Philadelphia: Chelsea House Publishers.
Ruoff, A. L. B. (1991). *Literature of the American Indian.* Philadelphia: Chelsea House
     Publishers.

(continued)

Simmons, W. S. (1989). *The Narragansett.* Philadelphia: Chelsea House Publishers.

Slapin, B., & Seale, D. (Eds.). (1992). *Through Indian eyes.* Philadelphia: New Society Publishers.

Snow, D. R. (1989). *The archaeology of North America.* Philadelphia: Chelsea House Publishers.

Tanner, H. H. (1992). *The Ojibwa.* Philadelphia: Chelsea House Publishers.

Trafzer, C. E. (1990). *The Chinook.* Philadelphia: Chelsea House Publishers.

Trafzer, C. E. (1992). *The Nez Perce.* Philadelphia: Chelsea House Publishers.

Waldman, C. (1994). *Timelines of Native American history.* New York: Prentice Hall, Inc.

Wilson, T. P. (1988). *The Osage.* Philadelphia: Chelsea House Publishers.

Wunder, J. R. (1989). *The Kiowa.* Philadelphia: Chelsea House Publishers.

LITERATURE SYNOPSIS GRADING CRITERIA

Team Members: **Date:** _____

_____   **Section:** _____

_____   **Score:** _____

_____

_____

Introduction

    Accurate background information is documented.   (5) _____

Literature Synopsis

    Key events are identified.   (2) _____
    Key events are interpreted.   (2) _____
    Logical conclusions are drawn.   (2) _____
    Influences are described.   (2) _____
    Contributions are described.   (2) _____

Composition

    The composition shows good mechanics, grammar, and spelling.   (1) _____
    The composition reflects clear, concise expression.   (1) _____

Bibliography

    Bibliography is presented in the correct format.   (2) _____

Delegation of Responsibility

    Work is fairly distributed.   (1) _____

Total   (20) _____

Comments

LITERATURE SYNOPSIS GUIDESHEET

The literature synopsis consists of four to six typed pages of text containing the following sections.

Introduction

The introduction provides the background information that the reader of the paper needs to know to understand the content. It is written from an objective viewpoint and supported with library resources. In this section of the paper, discuss some of the following issues:

- What do historians hypothesize about the origins of the Native American nations and their migration to the geographic location?
- How has the culture changed with the passage of time and what were the factors that influenced these changes?

Synopsis

The synopsis contains an analytical summary of the biographical content. It is written from the reader's point of view. It answers the following questions:

- What was the relationship between the Nation's environment and spiritual beliefs? How did these beliefs affect family roles, governance, rituals, and customs?
- What caused the clash of cultures between the objectives of the government or explorers and the objectives of the Indian Nation? What positive or negative effects resulted from this interaction?
- How was the Native American Nation changed? How was the government or explorer changed? Which characteristics or contributions have been integrated into the culture of the Native Americans? What coping strategies did the Nation use to resist the change?

Bibliography

The bibliography lists information about the source materials used in writing the paper. It is written in APA format.

Delegation of Responsibilities

In this section, describe how your group worked together in completing the assignment.

CHAPTER

10

UNIT FRAMEWORK: BLACK AMERICANS OF ACHIEVEMENT— 1860–1920

The United States is home to people of almost every race, religion, and nationality. Some, like Native Americans, have been here for thousands of years. Others, who arrived later, came in the hope of finding riches, adventure, and a new life. And some, fleeing war, famine, and persecution, sought only safety and a chance to survive. Black people alone were brought here unwillingly, stolen from their homes, and forced to live as slaves.

In spite of this cruel beginning, Black Americans have played a major role in defining and shaping American beliefs, traditions, and customs. From the beginning, they have helped to ensure the nation's security and economic well being. They are among the earliest explorers and were among the first people to expand and settle the frontier. Many of the men and women overcame incredible hardships with little to sustain them but their own courage and determination. Many others tried but were crushed under the wheels of unremitting repression and will never be known. Some did survive; some did triumph.

Like other racial, religious, and ethnic groups, Black Americans have made their presence felt in many fields—science and industry, literature, education, religion, and the arts. Yet it may be that the main contribution of Black Americans has not been in any specific area but rather to democracy itself. For in the struggle to secure, protect, and defend their own rights, Black Americans have helped to guarantee the rights of everyone else.

Altman, S. (1989). *Extraordinary black Americans.* Chicago: Children's Press.

RELEVANCE OF THE THEME TO TEACHERS

Throughout our history, the sacrifices, suffering, and triumphs of Black Americans have played an important role in shaping the nation and improving the quality of life of all Americans. In reading about the lives of Black leaders, students experience a respect for the courage that inspired these heroes to rise to leadership in a period when status was denied and discrimination was rampant. Both educators and elementary students benefit from exploring the motivation that drove these individuals to follow their dreams.

HISTORICAL BACKGROUND

The end of the Civil War in 1864 raised many questions regarding the citizenship of Black people who were no longer slaves. Would Black Americans be allowed the same rights as White citizens? Should Black males be allowed to vote, to hold office, or to own property? The Fourteenth and Fifteenth Amendments to the Constitution provided one answer to these questions: they gave to freed men all of the rights of American citizenship, including the right to vote.

But constitutional principle was one thing and the southern practice another. Through intimidation and violence, southern Whites sought to maintain the old system of racial domination and White supremacy that had prevailed in the prewar south. Throughout the region, Blacks were beaten for attempting to vote, Black political leaders were assassinated, and the Ku Klux Klan was organized with the object of keeping Blacks "in their place." By the late 1860s, it was clear that White southerners were determined to prevent any change in their system of racial privilege and power.

However, the history of Reconstruction was not only a story of Black suppression and White domination. Wherever they could, freed people reestablished the family and kinship ties they had lost during slavery. Meanwhile, thousands of ex-slaves flocked to urban areas in search of employment, and others purchased land and livestock in order to establish their economic independence. Most importantly, with citizenship rights guaranteed by the Constitution and the Union Army, southern Blacks eagerly embraced politics as a means to gain an equal place for themselves in American society. Form a series of Black political conventions held in the early years of the Reconstruction emerged a group of local Black leaders who spoke for the rights of freed men not only to economic opportunity and political and legal equity, but also to the possession of confiscated Confederate land.

Foner, E. (1994). Black reconstruction leaders at the grassroots. In G. B. Nash & R. Schultz (Eds.), *Retracing the past: Readings in the history of the American people* (p. 4). New York: HarperCollins. Reprinted with permission.

BLACK AMERICANS OF ACHIEVEMENT

RESEARCH TOPIC SIGN-UP SHEET

List the members of your group and your section with your research subject.

A. Philip Randolph
labor leader

_____

_____

_____

_____

Adam Clayton Powell
political leader

_____

_____

_____

_____

Billie Holiday
singer

_____

_____

_____

_____

Booker T. Washington
educator

_____

_____

_____

_____

Charlie Parker
musician

_____

_____

_____

_____

(continued)

(continued)

Chester Himes
poet

_____

_____

_____

_____

Count Basie
bandleader and composer

_____

_____

_____

_____

Dizzy Gillespie
musician

_____

_____

_____

_____

Duke Ellington
band leader and composer

_____

_____

_____

_____

Elijah Muhammad
religious leader

_____

_____

_____

_____

Ella Fitzgerald
singer

_____

_____

_____

_____

(continued)

Frederick Douglass
abolitionist editor

_____

_____

_____

Geroge Washington Carver
botanist

_____

_____

_____

Harriet Tubman
antislavery activist

_____

_____

_____

James Beckwourth
educator

_____

_____

_____

Scott Joplin
composer

_____

_____

_____

James Weldon Johnson
author

_____

_____

_____

(continued)

(continued)

Langston Hughes
poet

_____

_____

_____

Louis Armstrong
musician

_____

_____

_____

Madam C. J. Walker
entrepeneur

_____

_____

_____

Marcus Garvey
black nationalist leader

_____

_____

_____

Mary McLeod Bethune
educator

_____

_____

_____

Matthew Henson
Arctic explorer

_____

_____

_____

(continued)

Paul Lawrence Dunbar
poet

_____

_____

_____

_____

Paul Robeson
singer and actor

_____

_____

_____

Ralph Ellison
author

_____

_____

_____

Lewis Latimer
scientist

_____

_____

_____

_____

BLACK AMERICANS OF ACHIEVEMENT

BIBLIOGRAPHY

Adair, G., Huggins, N. I., & King, C. S. (1989). *George Washington Carver: Botanist.* Philadelphia: Chelsea House Publishers

Bishop, J., Huggins, N. I., & King, C. S. (1988). *Ralph Ellison: Author.* Philadelphia: Chelsea House Publishers.

Bisson, T., Huggins, N. I., & King, C. S. (1991). *Harriet Tubman: Antislavery activist.* Philadelphia: Chelsea House Publishers.

Bundles, A., Huggins, N. I., & King, C. S. (1992). *Madam C. J. Walker.* Philadelphia: Chelsea House Publisher.

Dolan, S. (1991). *Matthew Henson: Arctic explorer.* Philadelphia: Chelsea House Publisher.

Dolan, S., Huggins, N. I., & King, C. S. (1992). *James Beckwourth: Educator.* Philadelphia: Chelsea House Publishers.

Gentry, T., Huggins, N. I., & King, C. S. (1989). *Paul Lawrence Dunbar: Poet.* Philadelphia: Chelsea House Publishers.

Gentry, T. Huggins, N. I., & King, C. S. (1994). *Dizzy Gillespie: Musician.* Philadelphia: Chelsea House Publishers.

Gilman, M., Huggins, N. I., & King, C. S. (1988). *Matthew Henson: Explorer.* Philadelphia: Chelsea House Publishers.

Frankl, R., Huggins, N. I., & King, C. S. (1988). *Duke Ellington: Bandleader and composer.* Philadelphia: Chelsea House Publishers.

Frankl, R., Huggins, N. I., & King, C. S. (1992). *Charlie Parker: Musician.* Philadelphia: Chelsea House Publishers.

Halasa, M., Huggins, N. I., & King, C. S. (1989). *Mary McLeod Bethune: Educator.* Philadelphia: Chelsea house Publishers.

Halasa, M., Huggins, N. I., & King, C. S. (1990). *Elijah Muhammad: Religious leader.* Philadelphia: Chelsea House Publishers.

Jakoubek, R., Huggins, N. I., & King, C. S. (1988). *Adam Clayton Powell, Jr.: Political leader.* Philadelphia: Chelsea House Publishers.

Kliment, B., Huggins, N. I., & King, C. S. (1992). *Count Basie: Bandleader and composer.* Philadelphia: Chelsea House Publishers.

Koslow, P. (1997). *Booker T. Washington: Educator and racial spokesman.* Philadelphia: Chelsea House Publishers.

Lawler, M., Huggins, N. I., & King, C. S. (1988). *Marcus Garvey: Black nationalist leader.* Philadelphia: Chelsea House Publishers.

Norman, W. L., Patterson, L., Huggins, N. I., & King, C. S. (1994). *Lewis Latimer: Scientist.* Philadelphia: Chelsea House Publishers.

Rennert, R. S., & King, C. S. (Eds.). (1993a). *Book of firsts: Leaders in America.* Philadelphia: Chelsea House Publishers.

Rennert, R. S., & King, C. S. (Eds.). (1993b). *Book of firsts: Sports heroes.* Philadelphia: Chelsea House Publishers.

Rennert, R. S., & King, C. S. (1993c). *Civil rights leaders.* Philadelphia: Chelsea House Publishers.

Rummel, J., Huggins, N. I., & King, C. S. (1989). *Langston Hughes: Poet.* Philadelphia: Chelsea House Publishers.

Russell, S., Huggins, N. I., & King, C. S. (1988). *Frederick Douglass: Abolitionist editor.* Philadelphia: Chelsea House Publishers.

(continued)

Samuels, S., Huggins, N. I., & King, C. S. (1988). *Paul Robeson: Singer and actor.* Philadelphia: Chelsea House Publishers.

Schroeder, A., Huggins, N. I., & King, C. S. (1992). *Booker T. Washington: Educator.* Philadelphia: Chelsea House Publishers.

Tannenhaus, S., Huggins, N. I., & King, C. S. (1989). *Louis Armstrong: Musician.* Philadelphia: Chelsea House Publishers.

Tolbert-Rouchaleau, J., Huggins, N. I., & King, C. S. (1988). *James Weldon Jonhson: Author.* Philadelphia: Chelsea House Publishers.

Urban, J., Huggins, N. I., & King, C. S. (1989). *Richard Wright: Author.* Philadelphia: Chelsea House Publishers.

Wilson, M. L., Huggins, N. I., & King, C. S. (1988). *Chester Himes: Author.* Philadelphia: Chelsea House Publishers.

LITERATURE SYNOPSIS GRADING CRITERIA

Team Members: **Date:** _____

_____   **Section:** _____

_____   **Score:** _____

_____

_____

Introduction

Accurate background information documented.   (5) _____

Literature Synopsis

Key events are identified.   (2) _____
Key events are interpreted.   (2) _____
Logical conclusions are drawn.   (2) _____
Influences are described.   (2) _____
Contributions are described.   (2) _____

Composition

The composition shows good mechanics, grammar, and spelling. (1) _____
The composition reflects clear, concise expression.   (1) _____

Bibliography

Bibliography is presented in the correct format.   (2) _____

Delegation of Responsibility

Work is fairly distributed.   (1) _____

Total   (20) _____

Comments

LITERATURE SYNOPSIS GUIDESHEET

The literature synopsis consists of four to six typed pages of text containing the following sections.

Introduction

The introduction provides the background information that the reader of the paper needs to know to understand the content. It is written from an objective viewpoint and supported with library resources. In this section of the paper, discuss some of the following issues:

- What events were occurring in the nation during the period of 1860 to 1920 that affected the status of Black Americans?
- How were families affected by these events?
- Describe the educational and employment opportunities available to Black family members at this time.

Synopsis

The synopsis contains an analytical summary of the biographical content. It is written from the reader's point of view. It answers the following questions:

- How was the biographical subject different from the typical Black American of the period?
- What person or event in the subject's childhood influenced this difference?
- How did the subject influence the period? How did the period influence the subject?
- What strategies did the subject use to overcome impediments to his or her ideas, craft, talent, or innovations?

Bibliography

The bibliography lists information about the source materials used in writing the paper. It is written in APA format.

Delegation of Responsibilities

In this section, describe how your group worked together in completing the assignment.

CHAPTER

11

UNIT FRAMEWORK: IMMIGRANT GROUPS– 1860–1920

Between 1815, when the War of 1812 had been settled, and 1860, when the Civil War began, more than five million immigrants from every part of the world settled in America. They came for a variety of reasons: to escape famine or political and religious persecution, the spirit of adventure, boredom, desire to start life anew, and the appeal of a "golden land of opportunities." They flocked in from Europe, they struggled in from Asia, and they were dragged in from Africa. Representing virtually every race, religion, and nationality, their history is tightly woven into the history of American development during that period.

The story of immigration restriction does not begin until Americans lost their confidence in their ability to succeed, and the middle of the nineteenth century represents the benchmark of Americans' confidence in their own institutions. America was a large land whose geographic frontier was still wide open; it needed people to build, and the belief in a historical destiny westward tempered and held in check such signs of xenophobic hatred as the Know-Nothing party. It was a time too close to the Revolutionary War for people to forget their revolutionary origins. While settlers and the Army were still fighting Indians, how could foreigners be considered not native?

The eventual restrictionist victory occurred when a variety of themes, widely divergent at their points of origin, and traveling along scattered tracks throughout the last third of the nineteenth century, finally came together. The growth of an industrial and interdependent America at the turn of the twentieth century spelled the beginning of the concerted move to keep America American.

Like most large-scale historical movements, the trends that converged were social, economic, political, and intellectual: fear of rising crime and urban decay, the financial depressions and panics which threatened labor with job loss and lower pay, the complex and daily battles for votes and the flesh-and-blood battles in war, and the new theories of evolution and human biology. All these themes, which have their own unique histories and effects, when combined brought about an end of the great migration to America.

RELEVANCE OF THE THEME TO TEACHERS

Learning about the past helps us interpret events in the present and predict events in the future. Teachers are responsible for teaching students to become good citizens. Well-informed teachers need to have a clear understanding of the history of our nation and the experiences of the many ethnic and cultural groups that had the courage and persistence to leave their homelands to become Americans. In learning about these struggles and contributions, both teachers and students gain greater respect and pride in our nation and its diverse people.

HISTORICAL BACKGROUND

Nearly twelve million of the sixteen million immigrants who entered the United States through New York between 1892 and 1954 passed through the immigrant processing point on Ellis Island, a small island southwest of Manhattan. Once a picnic ground for early Dutch settlers, Ellis Island served as the nation's main immigration station for over sixty years. At the height of its activity, Ellis Island, which came to be known as "The Isle of Tears," processed over one million immigrants each year.

Disembarking ship passengers were ushered into an enormous processing hall to be examined by immigration doctors and questioned by immigration officials. The doctors examined the voyagers one at a time, but because of the overwhelming number of people, they generally did not spend more than ten seconds on any one person.

After examining an immigrant, the doctor made a single chalk mark on that person's clothing to indicate a diagnosis. Those who were chalked with a symbol, such as E, H, Pg, X, or an X with a circle around it, were pulled from the line and held for further examination. These symbols stood for abnormal conditions or potentially contagious diseases. For example, E stood for eye diseases, H for heart problems, Pg for pregnancy, X for mental retardation, and X with a circle around it for insanity.

These were all conditions for which a person could be denied entry into the United States. As frightening and humiliating as the ordeal may have been for most people, less than 2 percent were denied entry. Those whose conditions were contagious or required special care were often held on the island in special immigration hospitals until they were well enough to pass the entrance requirements.

As soon as the applicants passed the physical, they were interrogated by immigration officials to determine how much money they had, what prospects they had for employment, and where they might live. If interrogators believed that an applicant might not be able to support himself or herself and had no relatives in the United States to help, they could turn a person back.

If an immigrant's name was misspelled on the ship's roster or if the interrogator could not pronounce it (which happened fairly often), the immigrant was legally assigned a new name—sometimes a shortened version of the original or a new name that was not even similar to the person's real name.

Hauser, P. (1997). *Illegal aliens.* Immigrant Experience Series. Philadelphia: Chelsea House Publishers.

IMMIGRANT GROUPS

RESEARCH TOPIC SIGN-UP SHEET

List the members of your group and your section with your research subject.

Jewish Americans

_____

_____

_____

_____

Irish Americans

_____

_____

_____

_____

Italian Americans

_____

_____

_____

_____

The Amish

_____

_____

_____

_____

Japanese Americans

_____

_____

_____

_____

(continued)

(continued)

Mexican Americans

_____

_____

_____

_____

Greek Americans

_____

_____

_____

_____

Chinese Americans

_____

_____

_____

_____

German Americans

_____

_____

_____

_____

Polish Americans

_____

_____

_____

_____

Russian Americans

_____

_____

_____

_____

IMMIGRANT GROUPS

BIBLIOGRAPHY

Bodnar, J. (1985). *The transplanted.* Bloomington, IN: Indiana University Press.

Bureau of the Census. *Historical statistics of the United States: Colonial times to 1970.* (Part 1, Bicentennial edition). Washington: U.S. Department of Commerce.

Catalano, J. (1996). *The Mexican Americans.* Philadelphia: Chelsea House Publishers.

Daley, W. (1996). *The Chinese Americans.* Philadelphia: Chelsea House Publishers.

Di Franco, J. P. (1996). *The Italian Americans.* Philadelphia: Chelsea House Publishers.

Dolan, S. (1997). *The Polish Americans.* Philadelphia: Chelsea House Publishers.

Federal Communications Commission—Job Corps. Immigration. In *Dictionary of American history.* New York: Charles Scribner's Sons.

Fisher, L. E. (1986). *Ellis Island: Gateway to the new world.* New York: Holiday House.

Freedman, R. (1995). *Immigrant kids.* New York: Puffin Books.

Galicich, A. (1996). *The German Americans.* Philadelphia: Chelsea House Publishers.

Israel, F. L. (1996). *The Amish.* Philadelphia: Chelsea House Publishers.

Kitano, H. H. L. (1996). *The Japanese Americans.* Philadelphia: Chelsea House Publishers.

Kroll, S., & Ritz, K. (1995). *Ellis Island: Doorway to freedom.* New York: Holiday House.

Lawlor, V. (Ed.). (1995). *I was dreaming to come to America.* New York: Penguin Books.

Magocsi, P. R. (1996). *The Russian Americans.* Philadelphia: Chelsea House Publishers.

Manos, D. (1996). *The Greek Americans.* Philadelphia: Chelsea House Publishers.

Muggamin, H. (1996). *The Jewish Americans.* Philadelphia: Chelsea House Publishers.

Perec, G., & Bober, R. (1995). *Ellis Island.* New York: The New Press.

Reimers, D. M. (1996). *A land of immigrants.* Philadelphia: Chelsea House Publishers.

Schimpky, D., & Kalman, B. (1995). *Children's clothing of the 1800's.* New York: Crabtree Publishing Company.

Thernstrom, S. (Ed.). (1980). *Harvard encyclopedia of American ethnic groups.* Cambridge, MA: The Belknap Press of the Harvard University Press.

Watts, J. F. (1996). *The Irish Americans.* Philadelphia: Chelsea House Publishers.

LITERATURE SYNOPSIS GRADING CRITERIA

Team Members: **Date:** _____

_____   **Section:** _____

_____   **Score:** _____

_____

_____

Introduction

    Accurate background information documented.   (5) _____

Literature Synopsis

    Key events are identified.   (2) _____
    Key events are interpreted.   (2) _____
    Logical conclusions are drawn.   (2) _____
    Influences are described.   (2) _____
    Contributions are described.   (2) _____

Composition

    The composition shows good mechanics, grammar, and spelling.   (1) _____
    The composition reflects clear, concise expression.   (1) _____

Bibliography

    Bibliography is presented in the correct format.   (2) _____

Delegation of Responsibility

    Work is fairly distributed.   (1) _____

Total   (20) _____

Comments

LITERATURE SYNOPSIS GUIDESHEET

The literature synopsis consists of four to six typed pages of text containing the following sections.

Introduction

The introduction provides the background information that the reader of the paper needs to know to understand the content. It is written from an objective viewpoint and supported with library resources. In this section of the paper, discuss some of the following issues:

- What type of aspirations did parents have for their children in the period from 1860 to 1920?
- What were the typical family and societal roles of members of your immigrant group during this period?
- What type of occupations were available to your research subjects?

Synopsis

The synopsis contains an analytical summary of the content of the core text. It is written from the reader's point of view. It addresses the following questions:

- What factors in your subjects' native country influenced the decision to migrate to the United States?
- Was this vision realistic and were most of the immigrants in the cultural group able to achieve their dreams?
- What impediments or discrimination did the families of your group encounter when they tried to fit into their new community?
- What coping strategies did the subjects use to overcome impediments to their ideas, crafts, talents, or innovations?
- How did the subjects influence the period? How did the period influence the subjects' culture?

Bibliography

The bibliography lists information about the source materials used in writing the paper. It is written in APA format.

Delegation of Responsibilities

In this section, describe how your group worked together in completing the assignment. Identify the roles assumed by each member of your group.

CHAPTER

12

UNIT FRAMEWORK: EXPLORERS OF DISTANT FRONTIERS

In the course of more than 3,000 years, man's explorations and discoveries have quite completely plotted the land and water surfaces of the globe. The history of these adventures continues to excite interest, even now when man has begun to explore beneath the planet's surface and to reach out into space.

Chronologically, the record of exploration and discovery has been rather spasmodic. The story began in the eastern Mediterranean with the Minoans, the Phoenicians, and the Greeks. Important events came at fairly frequent intervals down to the second century of the Christian era. Then, for more than a thousand years, there was little new except the exploits of the Norsemen and the travels of Marco Polo.

The great European drive toward expansion overseas really began in 1415 when Henry the Navigator, a Portuguese prince, established a kind of center for the development of exploration. Henry was only metaphorically a navigator, but he had great influence on chart makers and the men who did go to sea. Within little more than a century, Christopher Columbus' ships had reached America, Vasco da Gama's had set up trade with India, and Ferdinand Magellan's had encircled the earth.

The only subsequent seaborne exploration of prime consequence was that of Captain James Cook in the South Seas late in the eighteenth century. After that, the emphasis shifted to land exploration, particularly in Africa. Finally, the long searching of Arctic regions bore fruit in the twentieth century, as did explorations in Antarctica.

The motives for exploration have been varied and often mixed. Probably many explorers, ancient and modern, have had, along with love of gain, a lively curiosity about what lay beyond the next cape. Some were hunting new homes for surplus populations. Much significant discovery was a by-product of military campaigning or of missionary activity or colonial expansion. Scientific considerations became increasingly important as time went on, with societies initiating and often financing new projects. But more often than not there was a mixture of motives.

RELEVANCE TO TEACHERS

Explorers were risk takers who had the courage and persistence to venture into the unknown and in doing so changed the course of history. It was not easy to step into uncharted territory or to convince others that some risks were worth personal sacrifices. In examining the lives of these adventurers, teachers and students explore the factors that influenced the explorers' character development and discover the effect of their sacrifices on the quality of life today.

HISTORICAL BACKGROUND

Michael Collins discussed the roles of explorers in the past and predicted new exploration challenges by reflecting on his Project Apollo experiences.

It is difficult to define most eras in history with any precision, but not so the space age. On October 4, 1957, it burst on us with little warning when the Soviet Union launched Sputnik, a 184-pound cannonball that encircled the globe once every ninety-six minutes. Less than four years later, the Soviets followed this first primitive satellite with the flight of Yuri Garagin, a 27-year-old fighter pilot who became the first human to orbit the earth. The Soviet Union's success prompted President John F. Kennedy to decide that the United States should "land a man on the moon and return safely to the earth" before the end of the 1960s. We now had not only a space age but a space race.

I was born in 1930, exactly the right time to allow me to participate in Project Apollo, as the lunar program came to be known. As a young man growing up, I often found myself too young to do the things I wanted—or suddenly too old, as if someone had turned a switch at midnight. But for Apollo, 1930 was the perfect year to be born, and I was very lucky. In 1966 I enjoyed circling the earth for three days, and in 1969, I flew to the moon and laughed at the sight of the tiny earth, which I could cover with my thumbnail.

How the early explorers would have loved the view from space! With one glance Christopher Columbus could have plotted his course and reassured his crew that the world was indeed round. In ninety minutes Magellan could have looked down at every port of call in the Victoria's three-year circumnavigation of the globe. Given a chance to map their route from orbit, Lewis and Clark could have told President Jefferson that there was no easy Northwest Passage but that a continent of exquisite diversity awaited their scrutiny.

In the physical sense, we have already gone to most of the places that we can. That is not to say that there are no new adventures awaiting us deep in the sea or on the red plains of Mars, but more important than reaching new places will be understanding those we have already visited. There are vital gaps in our understanding of how our planet works as an ecosystem and how our planet fits into the infinite order of the universe. The next great age may well be the age of assimilation, in which we use the microscope and telescope to evaluate what we have discovered and put that knowledge to use. The adventure of being first to reach may be replaced by the satisfaction of being first to grasp. Surely that is a form of exploration as vital to our well being, and perhaps survival, as the distinction of being first to explore a specific geographical area.

The explorers . . . did not just sail perilous seas, scale rugged mountains, traverse blistering deserts, dive to the depths of the ocean, or land on the moon. Their voyages and expeditions were journeys of the mind as much as of time and distance, through which they—and all humanity—were able to reach a greater understanding of our universe. That challenge remains, for all of us. It is imperative to see, to understand, to develop knowledge that others can use, to help nurture this planet that sustains us all. Perhaps being born in 1975 will be as lucky for a new generation of explorers as being born in 1930 was for Neil Armstrong, Buzz Aldrin, and Mike Collins.

Collins, M. (1991). Into the unknown. In S. C. Dodge (Ed.), *Christopher Columbus and the first voyages to the new world* (pp. 7–8). World Explorers Series. Philadelphia: Chelsea House Publishers.

EXPLORERS OF DISTANT FRONTIERS

RESEARCH TOPIC SIGN-UP SHEET

List the members of your group and your section with your research subject.

LaSalle and the Explorers
of the Mississippi

_____

_____

_____

Lewis and Clark
and the Route to the Pacific

_____

_____

_____

Lt. Charles Wilkes and the
Great U.S. Exploration Expedition

_____

_____

_____

Marco Polo and the Medieval Explorers

_____

_____

_____

Pizarro, Orellana, and the
Exploration of the Amazon

_____

_____

_____

(continued)

Sir Francis Drake and the
Struggle for an Ocean Empire

_____

_____

_____

_____

The Viking Explorers

_____

_____

_____

_____

Vasco da Gama and
the Portuguese Explorers

_____

_____

_____

_____

Alexander Mackenzie and
the Explorers of Canada

_____

_____

_____

_____

Captain James Cook
and the Explorers of the Pacific

_____

_____

_____

_____

Christopher Columbus and the
First Voyage to the New World

_____

_____

_____

_____

(continued)

(continued)

Daniel Boone and the
Opening of the Ohio Country

Ferdinand Magellan and the
Discovery of the World Ocean

Jacques Cartier, Samuel de Champlain,
and the Explorers of Canada

John Charles Fremont and the
Great Western Reconnaissance

Zebulon Pike and the Explorers
of the American Southwest

Exploring the Pacific:
The Expeditions of Captain Cook

(continued)

The Great Polar Adventure:
The Journey of Roald Amundsen

_____

_____

_____

_____

Into Space: The Missions of Neil Armstrong

_____

_____

_____

_____

EXPLORERS OF DISTANT FRONTIERS

BIBLIOGRAPHY

Bernhard, B., Goetzmann, W. H., & Collins, M. (1991). *Pizarro, Orellana, and the exploration of the Amazon.* Philadelphia: Chelsea House Publishers.

Cavan, S., Goetzmann, W. H., & Collins, M. (1991). *Daniel Boone and the opening of the Ohio country.* Philadelphia: Chelsea House Publishers.

Coulter, T., Goetzmann, W. H., & Collins, M. (1991). *La Salle, and the explorers of the Mississippi.* Philadelphia: Chelsea House Publishers.

Coulter, T., Goetzmann, W. H., & Collins, M. (1993). *Jacques Cartier, Samuel de Champlain, and the explorers of Canada.* Philadelphia: Chelsea House Publishers.

DeSomma, V., Goetzmann, W. H., & Collins, M. (1992). *The mission to Mars and beyond.* Philadelphia: Chelsea House Publishers.

Dodge, S. C., Goetzmann, W. H., & Collins, M. (1991). *Christopher Columbus and the first voyages to the new world.* Philadelphia: Chelsea House Publishers.

Gaines, R., Goetzmann, W. H., & Collins, M. (1994). *The explorers of the undersea world.* Philadelphia: Chelsea House Publishers.

Goetzmann, W. H. (Ed.), & Collins, M. (1993). *World explorers.* Philadelphia: Chelsea House Publishers.

Haney, D., Goetzmann, W. H., & Collins, M. (1992). *Captain James Cook and the explorers of the Pacific.* Philadelphia: Chelsea House Publishers.

Harris, E. D., Goetzmann, W. H., and Collins, M. (1990). *John Charles Fremont and the great Western reconnaissance.* Philadelphia: Chelsea House Publishers.

Kennedy, G. P., Goetzmann, W. H., & Collins, M. (1991). *The first men in space.* Philadelphia: Chelsea House Publishers.

Kennedy, G. P., Goetzmann, W. H., & Collins, M. (1992). *Apollo to the moon.* Philadelphia: Chelsea House Publishers.

Langley, A., & Barnes, K. (1995). *The great polar adventure: The journey of Roald Amundsen.* Philadelphia: Chelsea House Publishers.

Langley, A., & Crompton, P. (1995). *Discovering the new world: The voyages of Christopher Columbus.* Philadelphia: Chelsea House Publishers.

Langley, A., & McAllister, D. (1995). *Exploring the Pacific: The expeditions of Captain Cook.* Philadelphia: Chelsea House Publishers.

Langley, A., & Pang, A. (1995). *Into space: The missions of Neil Armstrong.* Philadelphia: Chelsea House Publishers.

Moulton, G., Goetzmann, W. M., & Collins, M. (1991). *Lewis and Clark: And the route to the Pacific.* Philadelphia: Chelsea House Publishers.

Smith, A., Goetzmann, W. H., & Collins, M. (1993). *Sir Francis Drake and the struggle for an ocean empire.* Philadelphia: Chelsea House Publishers.

Stallones, J., Goetzmann, W. H., & Collins, M. (1992). *Zebulon Pike and the explorers of the American Southwest.* Philadelphia: Chelsea House Publishers.

Stefoff, R., Goetzmann, W. H., & Collins, M. (1990). *Ferdinand Magellan and the discovery of the world ocean.* Philadelphia: Chelsea House Publishers.

Stefoff, R., Goetzmann, W. H., & Collins, M. (1992). *Marco Polo and the medieval explorers.* Philadelphia: Chelsea House Publishers.

Stefoff, R., Goetzmann, W. H., & Collins M. (1993a). *The Viking explorers.* Philadelphia: Chelsea House Explorers.

(continued)

Stefoff, R, Goetzmann, W. H., & Collins, M. (1993b). *Vasco da Gama and the Portuguese explorers.* Philadelphia: Chelsea House Publishers.

Wolfe, C., Goetzmann, W. H., & Collins, M. (1991). *Lt. Wilkes and the great U.S. exploring expedition.* Philadelphia: Chelsea House Publishers.

Xydes, G., Goetzmann, W. H., & Collins, M. (1992). *Alexander Mackenzie and the explorers of Canada.* Philadelphia: Chelsea House Publishers.

LITERATURE SYNOPSIS GRADING CRITERIA

Team Members: **Date:** _____

_____   **Section:** _____

_____   **Score:** _____

_____

_____

Introduction

    Accurate background information documented.   (5) _____

Literature Synopsis

    Key events are identified.   (2) _____
    Key events are interpreted.   (2) _____
    Logical conclusions are drawn.   (2) _____
    Influences are described.   (2) _____
    Contributions are described.   (2) _____

Composition

    The composition shows good mechanics, grammar, and spelling.   (1) _____
    The composition reflects clear, concise expression.   (1) _____

Bibliography

    Bibliography is presented in the correct format.   (2) _____

Delegation of Responsibility

    Work is distributed fairly.   (1) _____

Total

                                                               (20) _____

Comments

LITERATURE SYNOPSIS GUIDESHEET

The literature synopsis is a 4- to 6-page typewritten text that summarizes and interprets the information you have gathered from the core text and library sources. Papers are used by elementary teachers to prepare elementary students for the exhibits. The synopsis is written in a standard format containing the following sections.

Introduction

The introduction prepares the reader for the paper by documenting the importance of the exploration project undertaken by the explorers. This section is written from an objective viewpoint and should be supported with library references footnoted in APA format. The following questions are provided as suggestions to be investigated:

- What was known or believed about the exploration site prior to the exploration?
- Why was the exploration a dangerous undertaking?
- What impediments did the explorers have to overcome prior to the exploration project?
- What persons, groups, or agencies supported the exploration?
- How did the explorers finance the exploration project?

Synopsis

The synopsis contains an analytical summary of the content of the core text. It is written from your point of view. Begin by developing a timeline of the exploration project and a map of the exploration site. In your summary, discuss some of the following issues:

- What problems did the explorers anticipate and what equipment did they have with them to aid their efforts?
- What unanticipated events made the project more difficult?
- How was the exploration project accepted by the culture of people in the region explored?
- How did the exploration findings benefit society?
- What changes occurred as the result of the exploration findings?

Bibliography

The bibliography lists information about the source materials used in the writing of the paper. It is written in APA format.

Delegation of Responsibility

In this section, describe how your group worked together in completing the assignment. Identify the roles assumed by each member of the group.

CHAPTER

13

TIMELINES AND TABLES

TIMELINE OF AFRICAN AMERICAN HISTORY, 1859–1920*

The period of 1860–1920 breached the void between Victorianism and Modernism. In this era, Americans struggled to adjust to changes in family roles, cultural status, career aspirations, political values, and technological advances. Designing interdisciplinary instruction is a creative process that is stimulated by understanding the historical context that affected the lives of the people living in the period.

The timelines in this chapter provide the historical backdrop for the research of the unit themes. Timeline entries are listed to provide education majors with information that can be expanded into readings, activities, and projects for elementary students.

1859   ***John Brown's raid.***   On October 16–17, John Brown raided the federal arsenal at Harper's Ferry, Virginia (today located in West Virginia). Brown's unsuccessful mission to obtain arms for a slave insurrection stirred and divided the nation. Brown was hanged for treason on December 2.

         The last slave ship arrives.   During this year, the last ship to bring slaves to the United States, the *Clothilde,* arrived in Mobile Bay, Alabama.

1860   ***Abraham Lincoln elected president.***   Republican Abraham Lincoln was elected president on November 6, 1860.

*The following works were valuable sources in the compilation of this timeline:

Lerone Bennett's *Before the Mayflower* (Chicago: Johnson Publishing Company, 1982), W. Augustus Low and Virgil A. Clift's *Encyclopedia of Black America* (New York: Da Capo Press, 1984), and Harry A. Ploski and Warren Marr's *The Negro Almanac* (New York: Bellwether Co., 1976).

Library of Congress, Rare Book and Special Collections Division, Daniel A. P. Murray Pamphlets Collection. *http://lcweb2.loc.gov/ammem/aap/timeline.html*

1862   ***Slavery abolished in the District of Columbia.***   Congress abolished slavery in the District of Columbia—an important step on the road to freedom for all African Americans.

1863   ***The Emancipation Proclamation.***   Lincoln's Emancipation Proclamation took effect January 1, legally freeing slaves in areas of the South in rebellion.

New York City draft riots.   Anti-conscription riots started on July 13 and lasted four days, during which hundreds of Black Americans were killed or wounded.

Fifty-Fourth Massachusetts Volunteers.   On July 18, the Fifty-Fourth Massachusetts Volunteers—the all-black unit of the Union army, portrayed in the 1989 Tri-Star Pictures film *Glory*—charged Fort Wagner in Charleston, South Carolina. Sergeant William H. Carney becomes the first African American to receive the Congressional Medal of Honor for bravery under fire.

1864   ***Equal pay.***   On June 15, Congress passed a bill authorizing equal pay, equipment, arms, and health care for African American Union troops.

The* New Orleans Tribune.   On October 4, the *New Orleans Tribune* began publication. The *Tribune* was one of the first daily newspapers produced by Blacks.

1865   ***Congress approves the Thirteenth Amendment.***   Slavery would be outlawed in the United States by the Thirteenth Amendment, which Congress approved and sent to the states for ratification on January 31.

The Freedmen's Bureau.   On March 3, Congress established the Freedmen's Bureau to provide health care, education, and technical assistance to emancipated Blacks.

Death of Lincoln.   On April 15, Abraham Lincoln was assassinated; Vice President Andrew Johnson, a Tennessee Democrat, succeeded him as president.

Ratification of Thirteenth Amendment.   The Thirteenth Amendment outlawing slavery was ratified on December 18.

1866   ***Presidential meeting for Black suffrage.***   On February 2, a Black delegation led by Frederick Douglass met with President Andrew Johnson at the White House to advocate Black suffrage. The president expressed his opposition and the meeting ended in controversy.

Civil Rights Act.   Congress overrode President Johnson's veto on April 9 and passed the Civil Rights Act, conferring citizenship upon Black Americans and guaranteeing equal rights with Whites.

Memphis Massacre.   On May 1–3, White civilians and police killed forty-six African Americans and injured many more, burning ninety houses, twelve schools, and four churches in Memphis, Tennessee.

The Fourteenth Amendment.   On June 13, Congress approved the Fourteenth Amendment to the Constitution, guaranteeing due process and equal protection under the law to all citizens. The amendment would also grant citizenship to Blacks.

Police Massacre.   Police in New Orleans stormed a Republican meeting of Blacks and Whites on July 30, killing more than 40 and wounding more than 150.

Founding of the Ku Klux Klan.   Ku Klux Klan, an organization formed to intimidate Blacks and other ethnic and religious minorities, first met in Maxwell House, Memphis. The Klan was the first of many secret terrorist organizations organized in the South for the purpose of reestablishing White authority.

1867   *Black Suffrage.*   On January 8, overriding President Johnson's veto, Congress granted the Black citizens of the District of Columbia the right to vote.

Reconstruction begins.   Reconstruction Acts were passed by Congress on March 2. These acts called for the enfranchisement of former slaves in the South.

1868   *Fourteenth Amendment ratified.*   On July 21, the Fourteenth Amendment to the Constitution was ratified, granting citizenship to any person born or naturalized in the United States.

Thaddeus Stevens dies.   Thaddeus Stevens, radical Republican leader in Congress and father of Reconstruction, dies on August 11.

Massacre in Louisiana.   The Opleousas Massacre occurred in Louisiana on September 28, in which an estimated two to three hundred Black Americans were killed.

Ulysses S. Grant becomes President.   Civil War general Ulysses S. Grant (Republican) was elected president on November 3.

1869   *Fifteenth Amendment approved.*   On February 26, Congress sent the Fifteenth Amendment to the Constitution to the states for approval. The amendment would guarantee Black Americans the right to vote.

First Black diplomat.   On April 6, Ebenzer Don Carlos Bassett was appointed minister to Haiti—the first Black American diplomat and the first Black American presidential appointment. For many years thereafter, both Democratic and Republican administrations appointed Black Americans to Haiti and Liberia.

1870	***The first African American senator.*** Hiram R. Revels (Republican) of Mississippi took his seat February 25. He was the first Black United States Senator, though he served only one year.
	Fifteenth Amendment ratified. The Fifteenth Amendment to the Constitution was ratified on March 30.
1871	***The Fisk University Jubilee Singers tour.*** On October 6, Fisk University's Jubilee Singers began their first national tour. The Jubilee Singers became world-famous singers of Black spirituals. The money they raised built Fisk University.
1875	***Civil Rights Act of 1875.*** Congress approved the Civil Rights Act on March 1, guaranteeing equal rights to Black Americans in public accommodations and jury duty. The legislation was invalidated by the Supreme Court in 1883.
	The first African American to serve a full term as senator. Blanche Kelso Bruce (Republican) of Mississippi took his seat in the United States Senate on March 3. He would become the first African American to serve a full six-year term. Not until 1969 did another Black American begin a senate term.
	Clinton Massacre. On September 4–6, more than twenty Black Americans were killed in a massacre in Clinton, Mississippi.
1876	***Race riots and terrorism.*** A summer of race riots and terrorism directed at Blacks occurred in South Carolina. President Grant sent federal troops in to restore order.
1877	***The end of Reconstruction.*** A deal with Southern Democratic leaders made Rutherford B. Hayes (Republican) president, in exchange for the withdrawal of federal troops from the South and the end of federal efforts to protect the civil rights of African Americans.
	The First African American to graduate from West Point. On June 15, Henry O. Flipper became the first Black American to graduate from West Point.
1881	***President Garfield assassinated.*** President Garfield was shot on July 2; he died on September 19. Vice President Chester A. Arthur (Republican) succeeded Garfield as president.
	Tuskegee Institute founded. Booker T. Washington became the first principal of Tuskegee Institute in Tuskegee, Alabama, on July 4. Tuskegee became the leading vocational training institution for African Americans.
	Segregation of public transportation. Tennessee segregated railroad cars, followed by Florida (1887), Mississippi (1888), Texas (1889), Louisiana (1890), Alabama, Kentucky, Arkansas, and Georgia (1891), South Carolina (1898), North Carolina (1899), Virginia (1900), Maryland (1904), and Oklahoma (1907).

1882	***Lynchings.*** Forty-nine Black Americans are known to have been lynched in 1882.
1883	***Civil Rights Act overturned.*** On October 15, the Supreme Court declared the Civil Rights Act of 1875 unconstitutional. The Court declared that the Fourteenth Amendment forbids states, not citizens, from discriminating.
	A political coup and race riot. On November 3, White conservatives in Danville, Virginia, seized control of the local government, racially integrated and popularly elected, killing four African Americans in the process.
	Lynchings. Fifty-three Black Americans are known to have been lynched in 1883.
1884	***Cleveland elected president.*** Grover Cleveland (Democrat) was elected president on November 4.
	Lynchings. Fifty-one Black Americans are known to have been lynched in 1884.
1885	***A Black Episcopal bishop.*** On June 25, African American Samuel David Ferguson was ordained a bishop of the Episcopal church.
	Lynchings. Seventy-four Black Americans are known to have been lynched in 1885.
1886	***The Carrolton Massacre.*** On March 17, twenty Black Americans are known to have been lynched at Carrolton, Mississippi.
	Labor organizes. The American Federation of Labor was organized on December 8, signaling the rise of the labor movement. All major unions of the day excluded Black Americans.
	Lynchings. Seventy-four Black Americans are known to have been lynched in 1886.
1887	***Lynchings.*** Seventy Black Americans are known to have been lynched in 1887.
1888	***Two of the first African American banks.*** Two of America's first Black-owned banks—the Savings Bank of the Grand Fountain United Order of the Reformers, in Richmond, Virginia, and the Capital Savings Bank of Washington, DC—opened their doors.
	Harrison elected president. Benjamin Harrison (Republican) was elected president on November 6.
	Lynchings. Sixty-nine Black Americans are known to have been lynched in 1888.
1889	***Lynchings.*** Ninety-four Black Americans are known to have been lynched in 1889.

1890   ***The Afro-American League.***   On January 25, under the leadership of Timothy Thomas Fortune, the militant National Afro-American League was founded in Chicago.

African Americans are disenfranchised.   The Mississippi Plan, approved on November 1, used literacy and "understanding" tests to disenfranchise Black American citizens. Similar statutes were adopted by South Carolina (1895), Louisiana (1898), North Carolina (1900), Alabama (1901), Virginia (1901), Georgia (1908), and Oklahoma (1910).

A White supremacist is elected.   Populist "Pitchfork Ben" Tillman was elected governor of South Carolina. He called his election a "triumph of . . . White supremacy."

Lynchings.   Eighty-five Black Americans are known to have been lynched in 1890.

1891   ***Lynchings.***   One hundred thirteen Black Americans are known to have been lynched in 1891.

1892   ***Lynchings.***   One hundred sixty-one Black Americans are known to have been lynched in 1892.

1893   ***Lynchings.***   One hundred eighteen Black Americans are known to have been lynched in 1893.

1894   ***The Pullman strike.***   The Pullman Company strike caused a national transportation crisis. On May 11, African Americans were hired by the company as strike-breakers.

Lynchings.   One hundred thirty-four Black Americans are known to have been lynched in 1894.

1895   ***Douglass dies.***   African American leader and statesman Frederick Douglass dies on February 20.

A race riot.   Whites attacked Black workers in New Orleans on March 11–12. Six Blacks were killed.

The Atlanta Compromise.   Booker T. Washington delivered his famous "Atlanta Compromise" address on September 18 at the Atlanta Cotton States Exposition. He said that the "Negro problem" would be solved by a policy of gradualism and accommodation.

The National Baptist Convention.   Several Baptist organizations combined to form the National Baptist Convention of the U.S.A.; the Baptist church is the largest Black religious denomination in the United States.

Lynchings.   One hundred thirteen Black Americans are known to have been lynched in 1895.

1896   **Plessy v. Ferguson.**   The Supreme Court decided on May 18 in *Plessey v. Ferguson* that "separate but equal" facilities satisfy Fourteenth Amendment guarantees, thus giving legal sanction to Jim Crow segregation laws.

        Black women organize.   The National Association of Colored Women was formed on July 21; Mary Church Terrell was chosen president.

        George Washington Carver.   George Washington Carver was appointed director of agricultural research at Tuskegee Institute. His work advanced peanut, sweet potato, and soybean farming.

        Lynchings.   Seventy-eight Black Americans are known to have been lynched in 1896.

1897   ***American Negro Academy.***   The American Negro Academy was established on March 5 to encourage African American participation in art, literature, and philosophy.

        Lynchings.   One hundred twenty-three Black Americans are known to have been lynched in 1897.

1898   ***The Spanish-American War.***   The Spanish-American War began on April 21. Sixteen regiments of Black volunteers were recruited; four saw combat. Five Black Americans won the Congressional Medal of Honor.

        The National Afro-American Council.   Founded on September 15, the National Afro-American Council elected Bishop Alexander Walters its first president.

        A race riot.   On November 10, in Wilmington North Carolina, eight Black Americans were killed during White rioting.

        Black-owned insurance companies.   The North Carolina Mutual and Provident Insurance Company and the National Benefit Life Insurance Company of Washington DC were established. Both companies were Black-owned.

        Lynchings.   One hundred one Black Americans are known to have been lynched in 1898.

1899   ***A lynching protest.***   The Afro-American Council designates June 4 as a national day of fasting to protest lynchings and massacres.

        Lynchings.   Eighty-five Black Americans are known to have been lynched in 1899.

1900   ***A World's Fair.***   The Paris Exposition was held, and the United States pavilion housed an exhibition on Black Americans. The "Exposition des Negres D'Amerique" won several awards for excellence. Daniel A. P. Murray's collection of works by and about Black Americans was developed for this exhibit.

Lynchings.   One hundred six Black Americans are known to have been lynched in 1900.

1901   ***The last African American congressman for 28 years.***   George H. White gave up his seat on March 4. No African American would serve in Congress for the next twenty-eight years.

President McKinley assassinated.   President McKinley died by an assassin's bullet on September 14, a week after being shot in Buffalo, New York. President Theodore Roosevelt succeeded him as president.

Washington dines at the White House.   On October 16, after an afternoon meeting at the White House with Booker T. Washington, President Theodore Roosevelt informally invited Washington to remain and eat dinner with him, making Washington the first Black American to dine at the White House with the president. A furor arose over the social implications of Roosevelt's casual act.

Lynchings.   One hundred five Black Americans are known to have been lynched in 1901.

1902   ***Lynchings.***   Eighty-five Black Americans are known to have been lynched in 1902.

1903   **The Souls of Black Folk.**   W. E. B. Du Bois's celebrated book, *The Souls of Black Folk,* was published on April 27. In it, Du Bois rejected the gradualism of Booker T. Washington, calling for agitation on behalf of African American rights.

Lynchings.   Eighty-four black Americans are known to have been lynched in 1903.

1904   ***Lynchings.***   Seventy-six Black Americans are known to have been lynched in 1904.

1905   ***The Niagara Movement.***   On July 11–13, African American intellectuals and activists, led by W. E. B. Du Bois and William Monroe Trotter, began the Niagara Movement.

Lynchings.   Fifty-seven Black Americans are known to have been lynched in 1905.

1906   ***Soldiers riot.***   In Brownsville, Texas, on August 13, Black troops rioted against segregation. On November 6, Theodore Roosevelt discharged three companies of Black soldiers involved in the riot.

A race riot.   On September 22–24, in a race riot in Atlanta, ten Blacks and two Whites were killed.

Lynchings.   Sixty-two Black Americans are known to have been lynched in 1906.

1908	***A race riot.*** Many were killed and wounded in a race riot on August 14–19, in Abraham Lincoln's home town of Springfield, Illinois.
	Taft elected president. On November 3, William Howard Taft (Republican) was elected president.
	Lynchings. Eighty-nine Black Americans are known to have been lynched in 1908.
1909	***The NAACP is formed.*** On February 12—the centennial of the birth of Lincoln—a national appeal led to the establishment of the National Association for the Advancement of Colored People, an organization formed to promote use of the courts to restore the legal rights of Black Americans.
	The North Pole is reached. On April 6, Admiral Peary and African American Matthew Henson, accompanied by four Eskimos, became the first men known to have reached the North Pole.
	Lynchings. Sixty-nine Black Americans are known to have been lynched in 1909.
1910	**Crisis *debuts.*** The first issue of *Crisis,* a publication sponsored by the NAACP and edited by W. E. B. Du Bois, appeared on November 1.
	Segregated neighborhoods. On December 19, the city of Baltimore approved the first city ordinance designating the boundaries of Black and White neighborhoods. This ordinance was followed by similar ones in Dallas, Texas; Greensboro, North Carolina; Louisville, Kentucky; Norfolk, Virginia; Oklahoma City, Oklahoma; Richmond, Virginia; Roanoke, Virginia; and St. Louis, Missouri. The Supreme Court declared the Louisville ordinance to be unconstitutional in 1917.
	Lynchings. Sixty-seven Black Americans are known to have been lynched in 1910.
1911	***The National Urban League begins.*** In October, the National Urban League was organized to help African Americans secure equal employment. Professor Kelly Miller was a founding member.
	Lynchings. Sixty Black Americans are known to have been lynched in 1911.
1912	***Wilson elected president.*** Woodrow Wilson (Democrat) was elected president on November 5.
	Lynchings. Sixty-one Black Americans are known to have been lynched in 1912.
1913	***Jubilee Year.*** The fiftieth anniversary of the Emancipation Proclamation was celebrated throughout the year.

Harriet Tubman dies.   Harriet Tubman—former slave, abolitionist, and freedom fighter—died on March 10.

Federal segregation.   On April 11, the Wilson administration began government-wide segregation of work places, rest rooms, and lunch rooms.

Lynchings.   Fifty-one Black Americans are known to have been lynched in 1913.

1914   ***Lynchings.***   Fifty-one Black Americans are known to have been lynched in 1914.

World War I.   War began in Europe.

1915   ***Booker T. Washington dies.***   Renowned African American spokesman Booker T. Washington died on November 14.

Lynchings.   Fifty-six Black Americans are known to have been lynched in 1915.

1916   ***Lynchings.***   Fifty Black Americans are known to have been lynched in 1916.

1917   ***World War I.***   America enters World War I on April 6. African Americans in military service numbered 370,000—more than half in the French war zone.

A race riot.   One of the bloodiest race riots in the nation's history took place in East St. Louis, Illinois, on July 1–3. A Congressional committee reported that 40 to 200 people were killed, hundreds more injured, and 6,000 driven from their homes.

NAACP protest.   Thousands of African Americans marched down Manhattan's Fifth Avenue on July 28, protesting lynchings, race riots, and the denial of rights.

A race riot.   On August 23, a riot erupted in Houston between Black soldiers and White citizens. Two Blacks and eleven Whites were killed. Eighteen Black soldiers were hanged for participation in the riot.

Supreme Court acts.   On November 5, the Supreme Court struck down the Louisville, Kentucky, ordinance mandating segregated neighborhoods.

Lynchings.   Thirty-six Black Americans are known to have been lynched in 1917.

1918   ***A race riot.***   On July 25–28, a race riot occurred in Chester, Pennsylvania. Three Blacks and two Whites were killed.

A race riot.   On July 26–29 a race riot occurred in Philadelphia, Pennsylvania. Three Blacks and one White were killed.

War World I ends.   The Armistice took effect on November 11, ending World War I. The northern migration of African Americans began in earnest during the war. By 1930 there were 1,035,000 more Black Americans in the North, and 1,143,000 fewer Black Americans in the South than in 1910.

Lynchings.   Sixty Black Americans are known to have been lynched in 1918.

1919   *"Red Summer."*   This decade of the Twenties witnessed the Harlem Renaissance, a remarkable period of creativity for Black writers, poets, and artists, including these authors:

Claude McKay, *Harlem Shadows,* 1922

Jean Toomer, *Cane,* 1923

Alaine Locke, *The New Negro,* 1925

Countee Cullen, *Color,* 1925

The rise of Marcus Garvey.   On August 1, Marcus Garvey's Universal Improvement Association held its national convention in Harlem, the traditionally Black neighborhood in New York City. Garvey's African nationalist movement was the first Black American mass movement, and at its height it claimed hundreds of thousands of supporters

Harding elected president.   On November 3, Warren G. Harding (Republican) was elected president.

Lynchings.   Fifty-three Black Americans are known to have been lynched in 1919.

UNITED STATES HISTORY: 1860–1920*

Basic Household Items

1872   First square-bottom grocery bag is invented in United States.

1877   Telephones (local services) are introduced.

1879   American inventor Thomas Alva Edison (1847–1931) demonstrates first practical electric light bulb in New Jersey.

1887   Well-to-do Illinois housewife Josephine Cochrane invents first mechanical dishwasher, after becoming annoyed at breakage of her fine china by kitchen servants.

1888   U.S. inventor John H. Loud patents first ball-point pen.

1888	Kodak markets its first home camera.
1889	Earliest electric oven is installed in Swiss hotel. It is available in U.S. in 1891.
1890	Aluminum saucepan is invented in Ohio.
1893	Early form of zipper is introduced. It is demonstrated at World's Columbian Exposition in Chicago.
1896	Earliest trading stamps, S&H stamps, are introduced in United States for redemption of merchandise.
1900	Paper clip is patented.
1902	First "teddy bear," named after U.S. President Theodore Roosevelt (1858–1919), is marketed.
1903	Safety razors go on sale.
1907	Chicago company develops "Thor," first self-contained electric clothes washer.
1908	Disposable paper cups are introduced.
1913	Brillo pads are commercially available.
1913	First home refrigerator is manufactured in Chicago.
1915	Lipstick is marketed for first time.
1918	First pop-up toaster is patented in United States. It is marketed in 1930.
c.1920	Home radios are introduced.
1920	New Jersey company, Johnson & Johnson, introduces Band-Aids.

Accidents in the Air

1907	Lt. Thomas E. Selfridge is first airplane fatality when plane he is flying with Orville Wright crashes in Fort Meyer, Virginia (September 17). Wright is badly injured.
1912	First U.S. dirigible, *Akron,* explodes over Atlantic City, New Jersey (July 2). Five perish.
1919	Dirigible crashes into skylight at Chicago bank, killing thirteen (July 21).

Train Wrecks and Auto Accidents

1864	Collision of Erie and prisoner trains at Shohla, Pennsylvania (July 15); 148 die.

Explosions and Mining Disasters Since 1900

1900	Coal-mine explosion in Scorfield, Utah (May 1); 200 die.

1904   Coal-mine explosion in Cheswick, Pennsylvania (January 25);
179 die.

1906   Coal-mine explosion in Monogah, West Virginia (December 6);
361 die.

1907   Jacob's Creek, Pennsylvania coal-mine explosion (December 19);
239 die.

1909   Coal-mine fire at Cherry, Illinois (November 13); 259 die.

1910   Los Angeles Times Building explosion (October 1); 21 die.

1914   Eccles, West Virginia coal-mine disaster (April 28); 181 die.

1918   TNT explodes at Oakdale, Pennsylvania chemical plant (May 18);
about 200 are killed.

Ship Sinkings and Other Accidents at Sea Since 1900

1904   Excursion steamer *General Slocum* burns offshore New York (June
15); 1,021 die.

1915   Steamer *Eastland* sinks in Chicago River (July 24); 852 die.

1918   U.S. naval vessel *Cyclops* disappears in Atlantic en route from
Rio de Janeiro to Baltimore, Maryland (March); 324 aboard are
presumed lost.

Natural Disasters

Earthquakes

1872   One of the largest quakes to strike California fractures earth for 100
miles.

1906   Total of four square miles of downtown San Francisco, California
are destroyed by earthquake and subsequent fire (beginning April
18). Quake measures 8.3 on Richter scale; more than 500 perish.

Floods, Tsunamis, and Tidal Waves

1889   Collapse of South Fork Dam causes flash flood to hit Johnstown,
Pennsylvania, killing 2,209 (May 31).

1893   Tidal wave generated by hurricane hits U.S. southern coast,
submerging islands between Charleston, South Carolina and
Savannah, Georgia (August 27); 1,000 die.

1900   Hurricane and accompanying tidal wave inundate Galveston, Texas
(September 8); 6,000 die.

Hurricanes, Typhoons, and Cyclones

1900   Hurricane and accompanying tidal wave strike Galveston, Texas
(September 8), destroying half the city's buildings and killing 6,000.

1906   Some 100 railroad laborers living on houseboats in Florida Keys are killed when hurricane strikes area (October 18).

1915   Worst hurricane of century to date ravages Galveston, Texas (August 16); 275 perish.

1916   Spanish steamer Valbanera disappears with 488 on board when hurricane strikes Straits of Florida (September 9–10).

1919   Major hurricane ravages Gulf Coast from Texas to Florida (September 14–17), taking more than 300 lives.

Snowstorms and Blizzards

1886   Kansas loses 80 percent of its cattle when blizzard ravages five mid-southwestern states (January 6–13); at least eighty lose their lives.

1888   "The Blizzard of '88" buries New York City and New England in snowdrifts up to 15 feet high (March 11–14); 800 people die, more than 200 of those in New York City alone.

1891   Iowa, Nebraska, and South Dakota are wracked by severe snowstorms with accompanying winds up to 80 mph (February 8); twenty-three die.

1896   Blizzard claims twenty-nine lives in Minnesota and Dakotas (November 25–28).

1909   Christmas blizzard ravages eastern United States, causing more than $20 million in damages (December 25–26); twenty-eight die.

1913   Snowstorms dump 35 inches in Great Lakes area of United States, wrecking eight ships on Lake Huron (November 7–11); 230 perish.

Tornadoes

1900   Damage of $500,000 is caused by six tornadoes that hit Alabama, Arkansas, and Mississippi (November 20).

1905   Tornado touches down in Marquette, Kansas, destroying town (May 9).

1905   Twenty buildings are leveled by deadly tornado in Texas (July 5). Hundreds of buildings are destroyed and sixty-four die as tornado strikes Arkansas (March 8).

1911   Tornado strikes Kansas and Oklahoma, leaving four towns in ruins (April 13).

1915   Savage tornado strikes Kansas, Nebraska, and North Dakota, creating swath of destruction sixteen miles wide (November 10).

1917   Large area from Illinois to Alabama and Arkansas to Tennessee is hit by many tornadoes (May 26–27); 249 die.

1917   Tornado in Indiana kills 45 and leaves 2,500 homeless (March 23).

1920 Eleven tornadoes devastate five Midwestern states, doing millions of dollars in damage. In Chicago, more than 100 buildings are destroyed.

1920 Series of tornadoes sweeps Mississippi, Alabama, and Tennessee (April 20); 220 are killed.

Volcanic Eruptions

1912 Massive and violent eruption of Mount Katmai in Alaska results in creation of Valley of 10,000 Smokes (June).

Plagues and Epidemics

1840–62 Cholera spreads worldwide; fatalities are in millions.

1889–90 Great influenza epidemic afflicts 40 percent of world; deaths are in millions.

1893–94 Renewed worldwide outbreak of cholera takes millions of lives.

1917–19 Influenza pandemic; estimates of dead range as high as fifty million.

Architecture

1871 Great Chicago Fire destroys much of city. Rebuilt city becomes center for modern American architecture.

1884 First modern metal-frame skyscraper, Chicago's 10-story Home Insurance Building, is designed by U.S. architect William Jenney (1832–1907). It features metal skeleton of cast-iron columns and nonsupporting curtain walls, which become characteristic of modern design.

1885 American architect Henry Richardson (1838–86), among earliest of U.S. architects to experiment with modern designs, constructs several buildings in Chicago. He successfully blends medieval Romanesque architectural elements in modern geometric style.

1890s Chicago School of Architects becomes famous for construction of modern steel-frame buildings and stores.

1900 U.S. architect Frank Lloyd Wright (1869–1959) becomes famous for designing houses in "prairie style," characterized by low, horizontal lines and use of natural earth colors. Wright believes buildings should complement settings.

Education

1861 First Ph.D. degree in United States awarded at Yale University.

1862 Federal land grants are provided to aid agricultural colleges in United States.

1867	First U.S. commissioner of education, Henry Barnard (1811–1900), begins term.
1873	Beginning of Chautauqua Movement in U.S. adult education.
1873	First public-school kindergarten is established in Missouri.
1874	Michigan Supreme Court upholds taxes for public high schooling.
1890	Educational testing is begun in some U.S. schools.
1896	U.S. Supreme Court decision approves "separate but equal" schooling, legal precedent for segregated schools.
1896	American philosopher and educator John Dewey (1859–1952) founds elementary school in Chicago to experiment with progressive education ideas.
1897	Founding of National Congress of Mothers, precursor of PTA.
c.1920	Establishment of first U.S. nursery school.

Development of Automobiles

1879	First U.S. automobile patent is granted, to George B. Seldon.
1893	First practical American automobile is built by businessmen Charles (1861–1938) and J. Frank Duryea (1869–1967). They begin manufacturing in 1859. Their second car wins the first U.S. automobile race, between Chicago and Evanston, Illinois.
1896	American businessman Henry Ford (1863–1947) produces his first car, two-cylinder "quadri-cycle."
1896	U.S. manufacturer Ransom Olds (1864–1950) builds his first car. He begins production of first Oldsmobiles in 1899.
c.1898	Several U.S. companies begin large-scale manufacture of freight-carrying trucks.
1900	Electric cars, despite their limited power, make up 38 percent of American market.
1901	Fire at factory of Ransom Olds leads to his purchasing car components from outside suppliers, making first step towards future mass production of automobiles.
1905	Society of Automobile Engineers is established in United States, encouraging standardization of auto parts.
1906	Stanley steam car travels at 127 mph in Florida race.
1908	Henry Ford introduces inexpensive, well-built Model T. It becomes enormously popular worldwide.

1914   Ford begins assembly-line production of Model T, further lowering its price.

1915   U.S. trucks total 158,000 (up from 700 in 1905).

1915   Ford's Michigan assembly-line factory produces over 500,000 Model Ts. Each sells for $440. Ford offers first car rebates on his Model T, $50.

1920   Four-wheel hydraulic brakes are introduced by U.S. Deusenberg company.

Photography

1861   Matthew Brady (1823–96) organizes first photographic coverage of actual combat in American Civil War. He and others hired by him help compile photographic record of this war.

1871   Dry-plate (with silver halide emulsion) process is invented. Coated plates are marketed by 1876.

1873   Photographic print paper (silver bromide gelatin coated) is introduced.

1878   First moving-picture technology emerges. Zoopraxiscope, step beyond earlier Zoetrope, cast series of photographs nonstop at viewer's eye.

1880   Anthony Company (now GAF) begins selling Eastman dry-plate negatives for photo images.

c.1880   Flash powder (magnesium and potassium chlorate) is used to create extra light for photographs.

1881   First color photograph is produced by Frederick E. Ives (1856–1937).

1885   High-speed photograph of bullet in flight is taken, using sparks to provide flash.

1887   Celluloid roll film is developed by Hannibal W. Goodwin (1822–1900).

c.1887   First leaf-type shutter is invented.

1888   Eastman Kodak introduces portable camera—$25 camera loaded at factory with 100-exposure roll of celluloid film. Factory later must unload camera and develop exposed roll of film.

1891–1903 Kodak improves celluloid roll film, introducing paper-backed, daylight-loading roll. It makes gelatin-coated film that allows easier handling and printing of negatives.

1900   Kodak introduces its first Brownie camera for children.

1920   Color camera with sensitized plates that reproduce color images is marketed.

Electricity

1876   American inventor Alexander Graham Bell (1847–1922) patents telephone, second great communication device based on electrical current. Telephone soon surpasses telegraph as primary communication system.

1879   U.S. inventor Thomas Alva Edison (1847–1931) demonstrates incandescent light bulb, constructed with carbonized cotton filament, in New Jersey. (Bulb introduced by British inventor in 1878 was unsuccessful.)

1880   First electric generating station, built by Edison in London, England, to provide power for street lights, goes into operation.

1881   Invention of improved storage battery.

1881   System for distributing AC current, allowing longer-distance power transmission, is patented.

1882   Modern three-wire system of electrical transmission is patented by Edison.

1882   First electric generating plant in United States opens in New York City, providing power for nation's first system of electric lighting.

1884   First electric alternator is invented by Croatian-born American Nikola Tesla (1856–1943).

1885   Electric transformer is invented.

1886   American George Westinghouse (1846–1914) demonstrates AC-current power system, revealing advantages over DC systems then in use.

1888   First AC motor is patented. Over next decades, it becomes efficient and widely used means for converting electricity to mechanical power for both industrial and home applications.

1890   First electric-chair execution takes place in New York.

1891   Tesla invents coil bearing his name; it produces high voltage at high frequency.

1891   First AC (three-phase) power transmission system goes into operation in Germany. First U.S. AC system begins service in 1896.

1900   First vacuum tube is invented. Discovery that electrons can be moved at great speeds through vacuum tubes begins electronic age.

1900s   During this century, electric ovens are marketed by c.1910; electric refrigerators by c.1913.

1904   First practical photoelectric cell is invented by Johann P. L. Elster.

1906	Tungsten-filament light bulb is introduced.
1906	American inventor Lee De Forest (1873–1961) patents Audion vacuum tube, which amplifies electronic signal. It becomes key part of electronic communications systems.
1907	Suspension-type insulators for high-voltage lines are invented, allowing transmission of much higher voltages (up to 150,000 in next few years) over longer distances.

Telegraph and Telephone

1866	Beginning of regular transatlantic cable service, connecting United States and Europe, after failure of first working transatlantic cable (1858).
1876	American inventor Alexander Graham Bell (1847–1922) patents his telephone, using one-piece transmitter–receiver that introduced current when spoken into.
1878	First telephone switchboard is in operation in New Haven Connecticut.
1878	Carbon-type-microphone telephone transmitter developed by Edison is on commercial use, making long-distance telephones possible.
1887	U.S. telephone companies by this time serve a total of 150,000 customers. From this time forward, telephone begins to replace telegraph.
1892	Automatic telephone switchboard is first used.
1893	Boston and Chicago are linked by long-distance telephone lines for the first time.
1894	Guglielmo Marconi (1874–1937) develops his prototype wireless telegraph.
1899	M. I. Pupin facilitates long-distance telephone transmission through use of loading coils (inductors).
1900	Wall-mounted model of telephone with separate ear piece and mouthpiece is introduced.
1901	First transatlantic radio telegraph transmission is achieved by Marconi.
1915	Researchers discover that vacuum tube successfully amplifies telephone voice signal, making cross-country and transatlantic telephone calls possible.
c.1915	Printing telegraphy using teletypewriters is replacing manual telegraphy in telegraph-company operators.

Age of Steam

1870s   Manufacture of early four-stroke gasoline engines begins. Development of powerful, lightweight internal combustion power plants (gasoline and diesel) marks the beginning of end of age of steam.

1880   Steam-powered plant for generating electricity is built in London (New York City plant starts operating later in year). Steam-generating plants soon become major suppliers of electricity for lighting and manufacturing.

1896   Unmanned steam-powered flying machines designed by American airplane pioneer Samuel Pierpont Langley (1834–1906) flies 0.75 miles before crashing.

1897   First Stanley Steamer is built in Massachusetts. By 1906 a Stanley Steamer, probably the best remembered of all steam cars, reaches top speed of 127 miles per hour. Steam cannot compete with quick starting gasoline engines in burgeoning automobile market, however.

Printing and Copying

1863   American printer William Bullock (1813–1867) invents first rotary press fed by continuos roll of paper.

1873   Remington Company begins manufacturing modern typewriter.

1887   Monotype typesetting machine is patented.

1904   American printer discovers offset printing by accident when he inadvertently transfers inked images to cylinder instead of paper.

1906   Photostats—photographs of documents—are developed.

1920   Dry offset printing is developed in United States.

Advances in Agriculture

1862   U.S. Congress funds federal Department of Agriculture and state colleges for agriculture studies.

c.1862   Steam-powered farm machinery, such as hay rake, is in use.

1892   First gasoline-powered tractor is built in Iowa.

1896   U.S. agricultural chemist George Washington Carver (c. 1864–1943) develops methods to make worn out cropland productive by growing peanuts and sweet potatoes.

c.1900   U.S. farmers use sprinkler irrigation.

c.1912   Number of farm horses in use begins to decline due to the development of improved gasoline engine. Number of farm mules begins to decline in 1925.

1917   Frozen-food process is developed in United States by Clarance Birdseye (1886–1956).

c.1918   Earliest crop dusting by airplane is recorded in United States.

1920   Power-operated elevators in barns relieve farmers of heavy work of loading and moving such things as seed bags and equipment.

1920   Several varieties of genetically bred, high-yielding corn are commercially available by or before this date. By 1960 more than 95 percent of U.S. corn is from hybrid seed.

c.1920   All-purpose tractors come into use, gradually replacing work animals and steam-powered farm machinery.

Development of Ships

1865–66   *Great Eastern* is used in laying first transatlantic cable.

1871   White Star Line's SS *Oceanic,* first modern luxury liner, is launched.

1872   Accurate sounding device is invented.

1874   Ocean liners cross Atlantic in seven days by this time.

1892   Great Lakes steamship *Christopher Columbus* is launched. It carries 5,600 passengers.

1899   *Oceanic,* at 704 feet, supersedes *Great Eastern* as world's largest ship.

1900   Steamship *Lusitania* establishes new transatlantic record of five days, forty-five minutes.

1909   Hydrofoil ship was invented.

1911   Gyrocompass is invented by American Elmer Ambrose Sperry (1860–1930).

1920   Steam engines began to be fueled by oil rather than coal.

Basic Technology

1862   American Richard Gatling (1818–1903) invents first machine gun.

1863   First rotary printing press fed by continuous rolls of paper is invented.

1863   First oil pipeline is built in Pennsylvania.

1865   Ice-making machine is invented by American Thaddeus Lowe (1831–1913).

1866   Invention of self-propelled torpedo.

1868	Celluloid is invented.
1969	First bridge made out of concrete is built.
1871	Dry-plate (with silver halide emulsion) photographic process is invented.
1873	Continuous-ignition combustion engine, basis of turbine engine, is invented.
1874	Ocean liners cross Atlantic in only seven days.
1876	Telephone is patented by Alexander Graham Bell.
1877	American Thomas Edison invents phonograph.
1879	Edison demonstrates incandescent light bulb.
1881	Improved storage battery invented.
1883	High-speed internal-combustion engine is invented.
1883	First dirigible that can be steered in flight is developed.
1884	Electric alternator is invented by American Nikola Tesla (1856–1943).
1884	Ottmar Mergenthaler (1854–1899) invents lino-type machine.
1885	Electric transformer is invented.
1887	Monotype typesetting machine is invented.
c.1887	Celluloid roll film is developed, making motion-picture photography possible.
1888	Adding machine is patented by American William S. Burroughs (1855–1898). In 1892 he produces machine that adds, subtracts, and prints.
1888	Eastman Kodak introduces portable $25 camera.
1888	First AC electric motor is patented.
1888	First ball-point pen is patented by American inventor.
1888	Gramophone, which uses flat disks to reproduce sound, is invented.
1888	Radial engine is developed. First-line cylinder engine also is built this year.
1892	First gasoline powered tractor is built in Iowa.
1892	Music is mass produced on records for the first time.
1893	Kinescope (peep show) for showing early moving pictures to single viewer is patented.
1895	William Roentgen (1845–1923) uses x-rays to photograph bones and internal organs of patients for first time.

1896	Successful model of diesel engine is developed.
1897	First turbine powered steamship, *Turbinia,* is launched.
1897	First Stanley Steamer automobile is built in Massachusetts.
1898	*Holland VI,* first successful military submarine, is built in United States.
1898	Magnetic recording system is invented.
1900	High-speed steel, containing tungsten and carbon, is developed.
1900	Wall-mounted model of telephone with separate earpiece and mouthpiece is introduced.
1900	First vacuum tube is invented.
1900	Electrical ignition system for internal-combustion engines replaces flame ignition system.
1901	Mercury vapor arc lamp is developed by American engineer Peter C. Hewitt (1861–1921).
1901	Safety razor is patented.
1901	First use of crystal in radio receiver.
1901	Marconi, using improved radio equipment, sends first transatlantic wireless radio message.
1902	Machine to liquefy air is constructed.
1902	Invention of first electrical hearing aid.
1903	Invention of electrocardiograph for diagnosing heart problems.
1903	Wright Brothers achieve first successful flight of heavier-than-air craft at Kitty Hawk, North Carolina.
1904	Invention of silicones.
1904	Invention of diode vacuum tube, rectifier tube that becomes important in electronic equipment.
1904	Flat-disk phonograph is introduced and becomes industry standard.
1904	First practical photoelectric cell is invented.
1904	Development of stainless steel.
c.1904	American printer accidentally discovers off-set printing.
1906	Light bulb with tungsten filament is developed.
1908	Invention of steel-toothed drill bit for drilling oil wells.
1908	Gyroscopic compass is introduced.

1908	American Henry Ford (1863–1947) introduces Model T.
1908	First electric distributor system for engines is invented.
1909	First totally synthetic plastic, Bakelite, is invented.
1909	Hydrofoil for boats is invented.
1912	First pressurized, submersible decompression chamber for underwater divers is built.
1912	Electric self-starter for automobiles is introduced.
1913	Geiger counter is invented.
1913	Regenerative radio receiver circuit for long-distance reception is patented.
1914	Red and green traffic lights are utilized for first time in Cleveland, Ohio.
c.1914	First commercial air conditioner is built by American Willis Carrier (1876–1950).
1915	Sonar is invented.
1915	Radiotelephony, long distance voice communication, is demonstrated, linking Arlington, Virginia, to Paris.
1916	Passive sonar system to detect noises coming from submarines is introduced.
1917	Freezing of foods is introduced.
1918	Active sonar, using pinging device, is developed.
1919	Introduction of short wave radio.

U.S. Labor Movement

1866	Workers in Baltimore establish National Labor Union (NLU) and work toward 8-hour work day. (NLU disintegrates in 1872.)
1869	Knights of Labor is founded. By 1886 it has 700,000 members and achieves some labor reforms.
1875	Strike by Pennsylvania coal miners called Molly Maguires, a secret and violent organization of Irish-American workers.
1877	Severe depression results in 80 percent unemployment of labor force.
1880	Term *boycott* is coined in Europe after British estate manager Charles Boycott (1832–97) is shunned by local citizens for refusing to lower rent during famine.
1881	Labor leader Samuel Gompers (1850–1924) founds Federation of Organized Trades and Labor Unions.

1886	Haymarket Square Riot (May 4) in Chicago is one of several incidents of violence linked to labor movement in late 1800s. It results in rise of antilabor sentiment.
1886	American Federation of Labor (AFL) is formed in Ohio to succeed Knights of Labor.
1890	Sherman Antitrust Act prohibits trusts that interfere with trade and is used chiefly against organized labor to prohibit strikes.
1892	Homestead strike by Pennsylvania steel workers erupts into violence when strikers shoot at Pinkerton detectives guarding strike breakers (July 6).
1894	Coxey's Army, about 400 unemployed demonstrators led by Jacob S. Coxey (1854–1951) and 6-piece band, marches into Washington, DC demanding federal help (April 30). The "army" disbands without success.
1905	U.S. Supreme Court rules that minimum-wage laws are unconstitutional.
1905	Radical union, Industrial Workers of the World (IWW), or "Wobblies," is founded to organize unskilled industrial laborers and to promote overthrow of capitalist system. The union, declining through World War I, is effectively crushed during postwar "red scare."
1916	Congress exempts labor unions from antitrust laws.
1917	Membership in AFL is now over two million; significant reforms have been made in salaries and hours.
1919	Steel-industry strike called by AFL leaders is broken by company strike-breakers.

U.S. Railroad Industry

1860	Some 30,000 miles of railroad track are in use nationwide.
1861–65	Railroads play significant role in warfare for first time in Civil War. They transport troops and large quantities of food, ammunition, and supplies to battlefront much faster than before. Union states hold over two-thirds of railway mileage during the war.
1862	Congress authorizes construction of railroad from Missouri River to California on central route, ending years of debate concerning five possible routes to the West. Union Pacific begins building westward; Central Pacific builds eastward from California.
1868	Air brake that can be controlled from locomotive is invented by American George Westinghouse (1846–1914) to replace hand brakes set on each car by brake-men. Westinghouse later invents automatic signal devices.

1869	First U.S. transcontinental railroad is completed. Driving Golden Spike at Promontory, Utah, marks formal completion of construction.
1870	Track mileage nationally exceeds 53,000 miles.
1874–76	Widespread railroad rate war causes rates to fall below amounts required to meet costs, leading to temporary truce among owners and traffic-sharing agreements in 1877.
1880s	Railroad building boom peaks. Over 70,000 miles of track are laid in this decade.
1883	Railroads adopt standardized time, with four zones each one hour apart. It replaces over 100 different railroad times that previously caused constant confusion.
1886	Railroads move toward standard-gauge track of 4 feet, 8.5 inches.
1887	Interstate Commerce Commission is created by congressional act to establish maximum railroad rates. Public demands federal regulation after numerous rate wars.
1887	Standard design for car couplers is approved following test of many models in Buffalo, New York.
c.1890	Conversion from iron rail to safer, stronger steel rail is largely complete.
1894	Strike by workers at Pullman Palace Car Company in Chicago. Over 25 percent pay cut in wake of Panic of 1893 results in nationwide boycott led by Eugene Debs (1855–1926). Strike is broken by federal troops.
1902	Record New York–Chicago run in twenty hours by *20th Century Ltd.*
c.1905	First electric lamps appeared on trains.
1917	President Woodrow Wilson (1856–1924) established Railroad Administration to control and coordinate rail services until end of World War I. Government control ends in 1920.
1920	Congressional Transportation Act encourages consolidations of railroads and establishes Railroad Labor Board to determine wages and working conditions.

New York Stock Exchange

1863	Official name, "New York Stock Exchange," (NYSE), is adopted.
1867	Stock ticker, device to telegraph and print records of stock transactions, is introduced.
1868	Memberships on NYSE go on sale for the first time, changing previous policy of lifetime memberships.

1869	"Black Friday" (September 24). Gold speculation leads to this financial panic. American inventor Thomas A. Edison (1847–1931) later invents improved stock ticker after watching tickers fail to keep up with this day's trading.
1871	NYSE abandons oral "call market" (in which president calls name of each stock and members bid to buy or sell) in favor of continuous auction market.
1873	NYSE closes for ten days following the Panic of 1873, which is caused by failure of several prominent New York banking houses and other firms.
1878	Telephones are introduced at NYSE.
1882	Two Providence businessmen form a company, Dow Jones, to provide hourly financial information.
1886	First day on which volume over one million shares is recorded.
1889	Dow Jones begins publishing daily newspaper, *Wall Street Journal.*
1895	NYSE recommends that member firms issue annual balance sheet to shareholders.
1902	Average closing prices of selected industrial and railroad stocks are published daily by Dow Jones. In 1929, list of public utilities is included.
1910	NYSE no longer trades in unlisted securities.
1914	World War I breaks out. NYSE closes from July 31 to December 11.
1915	Dollar is established as basic currency for quoting and trading stock.

The Developing U.S. Economy

1861–65	American Civil War. Wartime needs produce business boom. Railroad building after war helps maintain prosperity in North; South suffers period of economic chaos in postwar years.
1862	Federal government issues about $450 million in greenbacks as legal tender during Civil War.
1863	National Banking Systems is established.
1865	Taxes, enacted to finance Civil War, by this time account for 43 percent of federal government revenue. They include income tax and business taxes. National debt reaches $2.8 billion by this year, due to war time spending.
1866–94	Federal revenue exceeds public spending each year of this period. Public debt is nearly eliminated again.
1869	Government foils attempt to corner gold, resulting in Black Friday.

1873–78 Major business recession follows failure of Jay Cooke and Co. investment banking house, which marks end of prolonged speculative boom in railroad securities.

1870s J. P. Morgan emerges as a leading American investment banker.

1880s Investment bankers are active in financing extensive railroad bankers.

1890 Sherman Antitrust Act is passed. It becomes tool for breaking up monopolistic combinations during early 1900s.

1893–97 Business recession. Almost 500 banks and 15,000 commercial firms fail.

1897 Period of sustained prosperity begins. Minor setbacks aside, this period lasts through World War I and 1920s.

1900 United States adopts gold standard. $150 million gold reserve is to be maintained as legal tender.

1903 Federal government's Department of Commerce and Labor is created.

1907 Panic of 1907. Runs on banks force many closings due to insufficient reserves.

1909 More than two million Americans now own stocks as public interest in securities investment grows.

1913 Way is set for establishment of income tax by passage of sixteenth Amendment to Constitution.

1913 Federal Reserve system is established. It provides commercial banks with emergency source of funds.

1914 Federal Trade Commission is organized.

1914–18 World War I. U.S. business booms as the result of orders for war materials and U.S. participation in the war.

1916 Public debt is just $62 million prior to U.S. entry into World War I. It skyrockets to $26 billion by 1919.

1919 Business drops off sharply in immediate postwar years, but prosperity returns by 1922. Construction and real estate boom and consumer durable goods industry expands.

North America

1861–65 American Civil War ends.

1863 Emancipation Proclamation is issued by President Lincoln. It technically frees slaves in Confederate-held territories.

1865	President Lincoln is shot and killed by John Wilkes Booth at Ford's Theater, Washington DC.
1865	Thirteenth amendment to the Constitution is ratified, prohibiting slavery.
1867	United States buys Alaska from Russia for $7.2 million.
1868	Impeachment and acquittal of U.S. President Andrew Johnson (1808–1875) occur. Process is sparked by differences between Congress and president over reconstruction in the South.
1868	Burlinggame Treaty signed between United States and China.
1869	U.S. transcontinental railroad is completed with driving of Golden Spike at Promontory, Utah.
1871	In *Legal Tender Case* (Second), U.S. Supreme Court decides Legal Tender acts of 1862 and 1863, which fall within federal government's powers to meet emergencies.
1871	Great Chicago Fire, one of worst fires in U.S. history, destroys much of city.
1877	U.S. railroad building boom peaks. Over 70,000 miles of track are laid in this decade.
1880s	U.S. President James A. Garfield (1831–81) is shot and killed by disgruntled office-seeker.
1886	In Haymarket Square riot, anarchist bomb kills eleven during Chicago labor demonstration.
1896	In *Plessy v. Ferguson,* U.S. Supreme Court upholds separate-but-equal public school facilities for Blacks.
1898	In Spanish-American War, United States gains control of Philippines and Cuba.
1903	Era of "muckrakers" begins. U.S. magazine and tabloid reporters expose corruption in politics and business.
1903	In *Champion v. Ames,* U.S. Supreme Court approves federal powers to prohibit as well as regulate commerce, thereby establishing so-called federal police power.
1903	Wright Brothers achieve first successful powered flight of heavier-than-air craft, at Kitty Hawk, North Carolina.
1903	Hay-Bunau-Varilla Treaty grants United States rights to Panama Canal Zone.
1906	San Francisco earthquake destroys 4 square miles of downtown district.
1907	Democrats in Congress criticize government spending, which has doubled in past ten years to $1 billion per year.

1908	In *Danbury Hatters Case (Loewe v. Lawler),* U.S. Supreme Court rules against secondary boycott as restraining trade under Sherman Antitrust Act.
1913	Sixteenth amendment to U.S. Constitution is ratified, giving Congress power to impose taxes.
1914	U.S. Marines briefly occupy Veracruz after Mexicans seize U.S. ship in harbor there.
1914	Panama Canal, built by U.S. government, is opened.
1914–18	In World War I, Germany's unrestricted submarine warfare against merchant shipping helps bring United States into war on Allies' side (1917).
1918	President Woodrow Wilson presents his 14 Points, peace proposals advanced at Paris Peace Conference after World War I. One proposal calls for establishment of League of Nations, which United States later refuses to join.
1920s	Roaring Twenties period, postwar era in United States, is marked by economic boom, enactment of Prohibition (1920), and rapid social change.
1920	League of Women Voters is founded to educate women in use of their suffrage. Men are admitted after 1974.
1920	All U.S. states allow women to practice law by this date.

Major U.S. Supreme Court Decisions

1866	*Ex Parte Milligan.* Court limits power of military commission to try civilians in immediate area of war.
1895	*United States v. E. C. Knight Company.* Court sharply limits application of Sherman Antitrust Act (1890), thereby making federal control over monopolies difficult.
1895	*Pollock v. Farmers' Loan and Trust Company.* Court voids law establishing federal income tax, resulting in passage of the sixteenth amendment authorizing federal income tax.
1896	*Plessy v. Ferguson.* Court upholds separate-but-equal facilities for Blacks.
1898	*Holden v. Hardy.* Court affirms states' right to regulate labor conditions.
1903	*Champion v. Ames.* Court approves Federal powers to prohibit as well as regulate commerce, thereby establishing so-called federal police power.
1904	*Northern Securities Company v. United States.* Court revives Sherman Antitrust by finding in favor of federal government. In 1905 Court

upholds government prosecution of beef trust in *Swift and Co. v. United States.*

1908 *Danbury Hatters Case (Loewe v. Lawler).* Court rules against secondary boycott as restraining trade under Sherman Antitrust Act.

1919 *Schenck v. United States.* Court upholds restraint of free speech in wartime by Espionage Act. It applies "clear and present danger" test.

U.S. Constitution and Amendments

1865 Thirteenth amendment is ratified (December 2), prohibiting slavery.

1866 Fourteenth amendment is proposed by Congress (June 13) to ensure citizenship rights to former slaves and to prohibit Confederates from holding public office. It is ratified July 28, 1868.

1869 Fifteenth amendment is proposed by Congress (February 26) to ensure that right to vote will not be denied on basis of race, color, or previous condition of servitude. It is ratified March 30, 1870.

1909 Sixteenth amendment is proposed (July 12) to give Congress power to impose income taxes. It is ratified February 25, 1913.

1912 Seventeenth amendment is proposed by Congress (May 16) to institute direct popular election of U.S. senators. It is ratified May 31, 1913.

1917 Eighteenth amendment is proposed by Congress (December 18) to outlaw sale of alcoholic beverages. It is ratified January 29, 1919 and becomes effective in 1920, beginning 13-year prohibition.

1863 Nineteenth amendment is proposed to Congress (June) to give women right to vote. It is ratified in 1920.

IMMIGRATION PATTERNS 1851–1920

	1851–1860	1861–1870	1871–1880	1881–1890	1891–1900	1901–1910	1911–1920
All Countries	2,598,214	2,314,824	2,812,191	5,246,613	3,687,564	8,795,386	5,735,811
Europe	2,452,660	2,065,270	2,272,262	4,737,046	3,558,978	8,136,016	4,376,564
Asia	41,455	64,630	123,823	68,380	71,236	243,567	192,559
America	74,720	166,607	404,044	426,967	38,972	361,888	1,143,671
Africa	210	312	358	857	350	7,368	8,443
Australia & New Zealand		36	9,886	7,017	2,740	11,975	12,348
Not Specified	29,169	17,969	1,818	6,346	15,288	34,572	2,226

Report of the Immigration and Naturalization Service (Washington DC: Department of Justice, 1955), pp. 43–44.

INDEX

Aaronson, E., 21
Accountability, 4
Action research, 64–67
Aiken, W., 8
Alberty, Harold, 6
Amelia Earhart unit, 45–103
    appendices, 95–102
    assessment, 103
    bibliography, 103
    fact sheet, 58–60, 92–94
    historical background, 49
    integration statement, 89
    literature concept, 89
    literature synopsis grading criteria, 47
    literature synopsis guidesheet, 48
    materials, 46, 90
    motivation and, 90
    objectives, 89–90
    planning wheel, 50–53
    procedures, 90–91
    sample unit plan, 46–49, 89–103
    See also American Women of Achievement
        1860–1920 unit
American Association for the Advancement of
    Science, 4
American Women of Achievement 1860–1920 unit,
    28–43
    appendices for, 67, 69–76
    bibliography, 41–42
    grouping guidesheet, 35
    historical background, 29–31, 68, 71–73
    integration statement, 88
    motivational activities, 64–67
    procedures for, 67, 68
    relevance to teachers, 29
    research topic sign-up sheet, 36–40
    step book, 68, 74
    technology project, 68, 75–76
    United States History timeline, 159–179
    unit plan grading criteria, 32
    unit planning guidesheet, 33–34
    women's rights timeline, 31
    See also Amelia Earhart unit

Appendices:
    contents of, 67
    sample, 69–76
Assessment, 79–88
    defined, 81
    evaluation statements in, 87
    integration statement and materials in, 88
    normed and criterion-referenced data in, 81
    observational methods in, 81
    performance objectives in, 82–86, 87
    political implications of, 80
    standardized tests in, 7, 14, 81
    See also Grading criteria
At-risk students, 3

Basal readers, 5
"Basics" movement, 4, 5–6
Beane, J., 8
Beaudry, J. S., 16
Binet, Alfred, 14
Black Americans of Achievement 1860–1920 unit,
    117–127
    African American History timeline, 149–159
    bibliography, 124–125
    historical background, 118
    literature synopsis grading criteria, 126
    literature synopsis guidesheet, 127
    relevance to teachers, 117
    research topic sign-up sheet, 119–123
Blythe, T., 12–13
Brainstorming, 18–19
Brandt, R., 4
Brazee, E. N., 7–8
Brown, R., 16–17

Capelluti, J., 7–8
Carnegie Foundation, 2
Cassidy, W. J., 5, 6
Caswell, Hollis, 6
Chall, Jeanne, 5
Cognitive dissonance, 18
Collaborative learning, 7, 9, 19–21, 64
    See also Grouping

Comprehension, 16, 68, 70
Content objectives, 82–83
Cornett, L. M., 2
Criterion-referenced data, 81
Critical thinking, 11–22
    brainstorming and, 18–19
    classroom framework for, 12–13
    collaborative learning and, 19–21
    grouping configurations and, 20–21
    importance of, 12
    Socratic method and, 16–18
    visual literacy and, 15–16
Curriculum:
    design of, 13–14. *See also specific designs*
    integrated, 4, 6–8, 9, 14
    interdisciplinary. *See* Interdisciplinary
        curriculum
    national, 2–4, 9
    standards movement and, 2–4, 9

Davey, B., 21
Designing instruction, 63–77
    appendices and, 67, 69–76
    curriculum design in, 13–14. *See also specific
        designs*
    motivation and, 64–67
    procedures and, 67, 68
Developmental objectives, 82, 84–86
Dewey, John, 6
Discipline-based curriculum design, 13

Educational reform, 1–9
    integrated curriculum and, 4, 6–8, 9, 14
    standards movement in, 2–4, 9
    teacher education and, 2, 9
    teaching philosophies and, 5–6, 7, 9
Eisner, E., 2–3
Elias, M. J., 20
Evaluation statements, 87
Explorers of Distant Frontiers unit,
        137–147
    bibliography, 144–145
    historical background, 138–139
    literature synopsis grading criteria, 146
    literature synopsis guidesheet, 147
    relevance to teachers, 138
    research topic sign-up sheet,
        140–143

Fact sheet, 55–61, 87
    grading criteria, 57
    information sources for, 56
    purpose of, 56
    relationship of concepts to problem, 56
    sample, 58–60

Field-based instruction, 14
Fraley, R. C., 6
Frames of Mind (Gardner), 14–15
Freeman, Y., 5

Galambos, E. L., 2
Gardner, Howard, 14
Goals 2000, 4
Goldstone, B. P., 16
Goode, E., 21
Goodman, K. S., 5
Grading criteria:
    constructing, 46
    fact sheet, 57
    historical event project, 73
    literature synopsis, 47
    planning wheel, 53
    technology project, 76
    unit plan, 32
    See also Assessment
Gray, D., 17
Great Britain, 6
Grouping:
    configurations for, 20–21
    guidesheet for, 35
    See also Collaborative learning
Guastello, E. F., 16
Guidesheets:
    action research, 65–67
    constructing, 46
    grouping, 35
    historical event, 68, 71
    interview, 66
    library research, 72
    literature synopsis, 48
    reading comprehension, 68, 70
    technology project, 75
    unit planning, 33–34
    See also specific units

Harville, H., 6
Historical event project, 68, 71–73
Holmes Group, 2

Immigrant Groups 1860–1920 unit,
        129–135
    bibliography, 133
    historical background, 130
    literature synopsis grading criteria, 134
    literature synopsis guidesheet, 135
    relevance to teachers, 130
    research topic sign-up sheet, 131–132
    United States History timeline, 159–179
Individual differences, 14–15
Integrated curriculum, 4, 6–8, 9, 14

Integration statement, 88, 89
Intelligence:
    individual differences in, 14–15
    psychometric measures of, 14
Interdisciplinary curriculum, 11–22
    brainstorming and, 18–19
    collaborative learning and, 19–21
    components of, 12–13
    described, 13
    individual differences and, 14–15
    multiple intelligences and, 14–15
    nature of, 5–8, 9
    Socratic method and, 16–18
    theme selection for, 25–43
    visual literacy and, 15–16
Interview guidesheet, 66

Jacobs, H. H., 13–14
Jones, R., 5

Kendall, J. S., 4, 82
KWL charts, 65, 69

Lambright, L. L., 17
Lateral thinking, 18
Library research guidesheet, 72
Literacy:
    comprehension and, 16
    visual, 15–16
Literature synopsis, 46–48

Marzano, R. J., 4, 82
Mastery objectives, 82, 83–84, 85
Motivation, 64–67
Multidisciplinary design, 13
Multiple intelligences, 14–15
Murphy, S., 5

National Assessment of Educational Progress, 3,
    5–6
National Association for Core Curriculum, 8
National Commission on Excellence
    in Education, 2
National Council of Teachers of English
    (NCTE), 5
National curriculum, 2–4, 9
National Educational Standards and Improvement
    Council (NESIC), 4
National Middle School Association, 7–8
Nation at Risk, 2
Native American Nations unit, 105–115
    bibliography, 112–113
    historical background, 106
    literature synopsis grading criteria, 114
    literature synopsis guidesheet, 115

relevance to teachers, 105
    research topic sign-up sheet, 107–111
New Zealand, 5
Norm-referenced data, 81

Observational methods, in assessment, 81
Oral reporting, 68, 69

Parallel design, 13
Performance objectives, 82–86, 87
    content objectives versus, 82–83
    developmental objectives, 82, 84–86
    evaluation statements and, 87
    mastery objectives, 82, 83–84, 85
Perkins, D., 12–13
Philosophies of teaching, 5–6, 7, 9
Phonics, 5–6
Planning wheel, 50–53, 87
Political implications of assessment, 80
Procedures, 67, 87
    components of, 68
    sample, 90–91

Reading comprehension guidesheet,
    68, 70
Research. *See* Fact sheet
Rubrics, 46, 85
    See also Grading criteria

Scaffolding, 16
Schlechty, P. C., 2
Shannon, P., 5
Sinatra, R., 16
Sizer, T., 3–4
Skills-based approach, 6–7
Smith, C. B., 6–7
Socratic method, 16–18
Spencer, Herbert, 6
Spitler, H., 2
Stack, E. C., 6
Stahl-Gemake, J., 16
Standardized tests, 7, 14, 81
Standards movement, 2–4, 9
Step book, 68, 74

Teacher education, 2, 9
Teachers:
    collaboration among, 7, 9
    role in educational reform, 9
    teaching philosophies of, 5–6, 7, 9
Teaching for Understanding Project, 12
Technology project, 68
    grading criteria, 76
    guidesheet, 75
Thaiss, C., 6

Theme selection, 25–43
 characteristics of good theme, 27–28
 importance of theme and, 26
 project planning and, 26–27
 unit planning prototype, 28–43
Timelines:
 African American history 1859–1920, 149–159
 history of flight, 58
 United States history 1860–1920, 159–179
 women's rights 1860–1920, 31
Tredway, L., 17

Vance, V. S., 2
Vars, G. F., 6, 8
Visual literacy, 15–16

Wenrich, J. K., 6
Whole language approach, 5–6
Wilson, Pete, 5–6